IRISH ARCHITECTURAL AND DECORATIVE STUDIES
Volume V, 2002

IRISH ARCHITECTURAL AND DECORATIVE STUDIES

THE JOURNAL OF THE IRISH GEORGIAN SOCIETY – VOLUME V, 2002

IRISH ARCHITECTURAL AND
DECORATIVE STUDIES
The Journal of the Irish Georgian Society
Volume V, 2002

Published by the Irish Georgian Society
© Irish Georgian Society and the authors, 2002.
All rights reserved.

ISBN 0946846 960

This annual journal continues the publishing
tradition of the Irish Georgian Society's *Bulletin*
(38 volumes, 1958-1997).

Edited by Dr Nicola Figgis

front cover
Thomas Mitchell (attrib.), A VIEW OF KILKENNY,
c.1760 (detail) (courtesy NGI)

back cover and flap
The Honan Chapel, Cork:
– Detail of the St Gobnait window by Harry
  Clarke *(cover)*
– Carved oak pews, made by J. Sisk & Son *(top)*
– Detail of chancel floor by L. Oppenheimer Ltd
  (bottom)

Design   John O'Regan (© Gandon)
Production   Nicola Dearey
Printing   Nicholson & Bass, Belfast
Distribution   Gandon, Kinsale

Produced for the Irish Georgian Society by Gandon
Editions, which is grant-aided by The Arts Council

Gandon Editions, Oysterhaven, Kinsale, Co Cork
tel +353 (0)21-4770830 / *fax* 021-4770755
e-mail gandon@eircom.net
web-site www.gandon-editions.com

The Irish Georgian Society gratefully
acknowledges the grant-aiding of this book by

THE PAUL MELLON ESTATE

The Irish Georgian Society aims to encourage an
interest in and the preservation of distinguished
examples of architecture and the allied arts in
Ireland.

Further information – and membership application
details – may be obtained from:
THE IRISH GEORGIAN SOCIETY
74 Merrion Square, Dublin 2
tel +353 (0)1-6767053 / *fax* 01-6620290
e-mail info@igs.ie

IRISH ARCHITECTURAL AND DECORATIVE STUDIES

THE JOURNAL OF THE IRISH GEORGIAN SOCIETY – VOLUME V, 2002
EDITOR: NICOLA FIGGIS

———

Foreword

THE KNIGHT OF GLIN

This is our fifth *Journal*. We are again deeply indebted to the estate of the late Paul Mellon for the funding of this publication. It marks the new editorship of Nicola Figgis who takes over from Seán O'Reilly. Nicola is currently a lecturer in the History of Art department at University College Dublin, and has been well known for her research on Irish artists in Rome. She is about to embark on a study of the very important Irish artist, Nathaniel Hone the Elder. She was a collaborator with Brendan Rooney on the magnificent new catalogue, *Irish Paintings in the National Gallery of Ireland* (NGI, 2001), and we are very pleased that Brendan himself has been appointed administrator of the Centre for the Study of Irish Art at the NGI.

I think you will find this volume full of diverse topics. Freddie O'Dwyer continues his investigations into a new aspect of the politics and architecture of the Board of Works during the eighteenth and nineteenth centuries. Loreto Calderón and Christine Casey have identified a new plaster worker of the eighteenth century, and Jane Fenlon offers a detailed insight into the history of Bridge House in Kilkenny. We have two Italian-sourced articles: the altar rails at Monasterevin by Beatrice Whelan, and the two statues of Aeolus at Powerscourt by Patrick Bowe. Patricia McCabe shares her new research into the accoutrements of the Lords Chancellor of Ireland. No one has yet published an individual study of the Honan Chapel in Cork, and we are therefore delighted with Paul Larmour's contribution to this volume. Finally, we have a list of the recent acquisitions of the Irish Architectural Archive.

Let me repeat again that we welcome submissions of material from all scholars working in the fields of architecture and the decorative arts in post-medieval Ireland. And now the *Journal* has introduced colour printing, we can encourage more articles on the history of Irish painting.

Authors' biographies

PATRICK BOWE is author or co-author of nine books, including three on Irish gardens and *Gardens of Portugal*, *Gardens of Central Europe*, and *Gardens of the Caribbean*. He is currently completing a book, *Gardens of the Roman World*, commissioned by the J. Paul Getty Trust, California.

LORETO CALDERÓN worked for eleven years as librarian of the former Spanish Cultural Institute. Since 1997 she has worked as a freelance researcher on a wide variety of topics. She is currently carrying out a study of the members of the Dublin school of plasterwork.

CHRISTINE CASEY is a lecturer in the History of Art department at University College Dublin, and the author of many articles on Irish architectural history. She is co-author (with Alistair Rowan) of *North Leinster* (London 1993), volume 2 in the *Buildings of Ireland* series, and is currently preparing volume 3 on the architecture of Dublin city.

JANE FENLON is an art historian, and has published extensively on sixteenth and seventeenth-century Irish art and architecture. She is a contributor to the forthcoming *Encyclopaedia of Ireland* and *New Directory of the National Biography*. Her latest publication is *Goods and Chattels – A survey of 16th and 17th century household inventories in Ireland*, due in early 2003.

DAVID GRIFFIN is Archive Director at the Irish Architectural Archive. He was co-author, with the Knight of Glin and Nicholas Robinson, of *Vanishing Country Houses of Ireland* (1988), with Simon Lincoln of *Drawings from the Irish Architectural Archive* (1993), and with Caroline Pegum of *Leinster House: An Architectural History* (2000).

DR PAUL LARMOUR is Reader in Architecture at Queen's University, Belfast. His publications include *Celtic Ornament* (Dublin 1981), *Belfast: An Illustrated Architectural Guide* (Belfast 1987), and *The Arts and Crafts Movement in Ireland* (Belfast 1992). As a historic buildings consultant, he has carried out extensive research and survey work for the statutory listing of buildings in Northern Ireland.

PATRICIA MCCABE recently completed a doctoral thesis on the *Images of Law and Order, Accoutrements, Portraits and Memorials of Lords Chancellor of Ireland*. She lectures on the History of Art at adult education centres, and is also a practising artist.

FREDERICK O'DWYER is an architect and architectural historian with a particular interest in the nineteenth century. He is the author of *Lost Dublin* (1981), *The Architecture of Deane and Woodward* (1997) and *Irish Hospital Architecture* (1997). He has contributed a number of architectural biographies to the forthcoming *Encyclopaedia of Ireland* and the *New Dictionary of National Biography*.

COLUM O'RIORDAN is Archive Administrator at the Irish Architectural Archive.

BEATRICE WHELAN graduated from Trinity College, Dublin, in 2001 with a degree in History of Art and Classical Archaeology, for which she wrote her dissertation on the Church of Sts Peter and Paul in Monasterevin. Since then she has completed a Masters course in Multimedia Systems, and has produced a website on the church. Currently working as a teaching assistant in the History of Art department, Trinity College.

———

1 – No. 12 Merrion Square, Dublin (1764-68): stairhall

(Note that the wall colourings shown in this article are twentieth century.
The original shades would probably have been different tones of white and stone)

Number 12 Merrion Square: townhouse of the Right Honourable William Brownlow

LORETO CALDERÓN AND CHRISTINE CASEY

NUMBER 12 MERRION SQUARE, BUILT BETWEEN 1764 AND 1766 FOR THE RT Hon William Brownlow, is a little-known house of considerable scale and pretension. Brownlow (Plate 2) was a landowner, linen manufacturer, and MP for Lurgan, county Armagh, from 1753 to 1794. A respected and influential member of the House of Commons, he was narrowly defeated by a mere four votes in the election of Speaker in 1771.[1] Lord Charlemont described him as 'one of the most independent members that ever sat in the House of Commons of Ireland. Whenever he spoke, he was heard with peculiar attention and respect. To oratorial powers he laid no claim; but he delivered his sentiments with uncommon perspicuity, great neatness, great elegance, and occasionally, with a tempered fire and spirit, which were felt by everyone about him...'[2] Brownlow was also a musician of considerable talent, trained in Florence by the Abbé Felice Dona, and with his friend Lord Mornington was a member of the Charitable Music Society. He is reputed to have played the harpsichord at the first performance of Handel's *Messiah*.[3] Brownlow was twice married, first to Judith Laetitia Meredyth of Newtown in county Meath, with whom he had four children, and secondly to Catherine, daughter of Roger Hall of Narrowater in county Down (a first cousin of the Duke of Leinster), who bore him three sons and seven daughters. Three daughters by his second wife married peers.[4] Brownlow was a fastidious record-keeper, and his surviving papers vividly record the detail of domestic and business affairs in Lurgan and Dublin during the 1760s.[5] His building accounts for No. 12 Merrion Square expand our limited knowledge of domestic building in the city during the period. More importantly, however, by identifying the author of the house's ornate plasterwork decoration, they add a new and distinctive persona to the remarkable but largely anonymous Dublin school of plasterwork of the 1760s.

No. 12 was Brownlow's second Dublin house in less than a decade. The first, on Leinster Street, was built in 1755 at a cost of £2,000, and following the death of his first wife in 1764 was sold for £2,200 to the Bishop of Clogher.[6] In April 1764

2 – Engraved portrait of William Brownlow by Charles Howard Hodges (after Gilbert Stuart)
(courtesy National Gallery of Ireland)

the foundations of No. 12 Merrion Square were dug. During the next two years payments were made through a Mr Welldon to Wall the bricklayer, Morgan, stonecarver, Gilliard, carpenter, and Clement, bricklayer, and 721 feet of window glass was provided by Turner & Lilly of London. Between April 1764 and December 1765, £3,205 18s was spent on the house. On his marriage to Catherine Hall in 1765, the house was at an advanced stage of construction, and, after travelling in France, the couple took up residence at Merrion Square in 1766.

Brownlow was the second owner-occupier to build on the square. The first ten 'lotts' on the north side were taken by a group of tradesmen and surveyors who built a row of houses of varying dimensions and plans. Though John Ferrar's *View of Dublin* of 1796 attributes a design for the square to John Ensor and Ralph Ward, there is no evidence to support this claim, and the surviving documentation suggests that Lord Fitzwilliam had no architectural pretensions for the square other than that the houses be 'good and substantial ... three stories and a half high above the cellars', with a front area of eight feet and a flagged pavement of ten.[7] In November 1764, the engineer Charles Vallancey reproached Fitzwilliam because a level had not been struck for the houses on the north side, and each builder raised 'his street door and his attics without rule or guide'.[8]

While there is considerable variety in the door, window and parapet levels, the north side of the square is remarkable by Dublin standards in that most of the houses have granite rustication to the hall floor. This was evidently not the result of obligatory building clauses, and may reflect a standard promoted by Fitzwilliam, who provided lessees with stone from his quarries at a reduced price. He did, however, insist on unbroken terraces, and refused permission to open carriage arches to several distinguished prospective buyers. Brownlow's neighbour at No. 11, Columbine Lee Carré, was the first owner to construct his own residence on the square – a four-bay house which is considerably larger than Nos 1 to 9. Surprisingly, given the increase in scale, the front is of plain brick with no stone embellishment other than a Doric doorcase. Brownlow followed suit, eschewing the rustication employed in the adjacent speculative building and opting for a plain front of stock brick.

The site was a little under 70ft in breadth, and on it Brownlow built a house of 44ft and a carriage arch of 24ft. In February 1766 the coach-house lane was gravelled at a cost of fifteen shillings. Significantly, Brownlow was the only leaseholder to obtain permission from Fitzwilliam to construct a carriage arch. His friend and fellow musician Lord Mornington cited this favour in an unsuccessful bid to gain frontage on the south side of the square, flanked by two carriage arches. No. 12 is larger than all other houses on the north side of the square, and the interior is palatial in scale and decoration. A three-bay house over 44ft in breadth allowed for generous proportions. The plan, however, is the standard two rooms flanked by a hall and entrance hall. A long narrow concealed space flanks the entire east wall, and originally contained a service stair to the rear. This attenuated compartment is decidedly odd, and suggests perhaps that Brownlow intended to build a larger house of four or even five bays, but changed his mind mid-stream. This hypothesis is supported by the presence of an eighteenth-century basement vaulting under No. 13 – a narrow nineteenth-century house built on the site of Brownlow's coveted carriage arch.[9] Certainly the scale and grandeur of the interior sits oddly with a two-room plan.

The single-bay entrance hall is exceptionally broad and tall, and is the only

*3 – Doorcase on
first-floor landing*

opposite
*4, 5 – No. 12
Merrion Square:
detail of the stairhall
plasterwork
ornament by James
Byrne*

*(all photographs by
David Davison unless
otherwise stated)*

hall in a Dublin terraced house to have an Ionic pilaster order. The stairhall (Plate 1) is lit by an enormous round-headed window, the glazing now altered but retaining its carved frame with remarkably high-relief soffit decoration. The walls have large rectilinear panels with large and idiosyncratic birds perched on acanthus scrolls, and floral festoons and pendants (Plates 4, 5). While the window frame is Corinthian, the entablature is of an enriched Doric order with gigantic flowers in the metopes. Above the three pedimented doorcases on the first-floor landing are stucco over-door panels with vine festoons, while between the large wall panels and the doors are frameless pendants of fruit and flowers suspended from fictive ribbons (Plate 3). This spectacular if somewhat gauche plasterwork scheme was the work of James Byrne, who in 1765 was paid just over £446 for plasterwork in the house. This sum included the purchase and carriage of coals, and payments to Tim Mahon for lime burning, Robert Wheeler for nails, and Byrne's workmen for labour. Brownlow was evidently well pleased, as on 15 May 1766 Byrne received £7 13s 8d as a 'present for doing his work well'. Though noting its elaborate and ambitious nature, the

Georgian Society Records were less appreciative, concluding it was 'late rococo of inferior design'.

To date, and following extensive research, no biographical information has surfaced on the plasterer James Byrne, who is not recorded by Con Curran. However, a number of plasterers with the surname Byrne are noted as appearing on the Freemen's roll – Edward Byrne in 1692 and William Byrne in 1727. A Michael Byrne, who was not a freeman, is recorded in 1785. All that may be said with certainty is that in 1764 James Byrne had been working as a plasterer for at least a decade, as he had also decorated the interior of Brownlow's previous house on Leinster Street.[10] That Byrne was within the circle of Robert West is also beyond doubt, as his work displays marked similarities to decoration in houses associated with West.[11]

The front ground-floor room of No. 12, possibly the original dining room, has similarities to its counterpart at No. 86 St Stephen's Green – a house long attributed to Robert West. The walls have large moulded plaster panels which, while plain in character, are undoubtedly related to a group of contemporary Irish interiors inspired by French rococo *boiseries*, including the dining rooms at No. 86 St Stephen's Green (1765-) and Charlemont House (1763-), and the saloon at Dowth Hall in county Meath (*c.*1765).[12] Brownlow's room lacks the narrow vertical panels and foliated embellishments of those more elaborate schemes, having large plain rectangular panels with gadrooned borders. The first-floor rooms at No. 12 have stucco ceilings which relate closely in style and decorative repertoire to contemporary stuccowork at No. 86 St Stephen's Green. The ceiling of the front room bears comparison with its counterpart at Newman House, having an outer arabesque border and an inner border of flower garlands and birds (Plates 6, 7). However, in contrast to the fluidity and sophistication of the ceilings at St Stephen's Green, Byrne's work displays a hesitancy in design and a fondness for rich and gargantuan detail. That said, the stairhall of Brownlow's house is undoubtedly one of the most opulent interiors produced by the Dublin school of plasterwork.

The upper floors of No. 12 retain eighteenth-century joinery and coved ceilings, but are now reached by a cast-iron spiral stair over the entrance hall, which replaced the original service stair. All of the eighteenth-century chimney pieces bought in Dublin and in London were removed in the early twentieth century. While no inventories survive to record the furnishings of the house, Brownlow's account books allow some measure of imaginative reconstruction.[13] Some of the furnishings were brought from Leinster Street, including a six-foot walnut four-poster bed, and perhaps some of the pier-glasses and Chinese chairs carved for Brownlow by Thomas Oldham in 1756.[14] Oldham, a cabinet maker in Moore Street from 1768 to 1778, was the principal supplier of furniture for Leinster Street, but appears to have been supplanted by Thomas Gunston at Merrion Square.[15] Wallpaper for No. 12 was supplied by John Gordon of Temple Bar, and mirror and picture frames by (Richard) Cranfield. The floors were covered with Wilton carpets, and the windows with damask curtains. Lustres, six-branch candlesticks, and three-branch chandeliers were brought from London. Between 1764 and 1766 payments were made for a range of household items, including a toothpick case, a silver writing stand, a kettle, a coffee-pot, a carnelian seal and silver cutlery. Green tea, chocolate and dried ginger were among the household food-stuffs.[16] The Brownlows evidently dressed well: Brownlow's petty cash book kept during a tour in France in 1775-76 records the purchase of embroidered silk waistcoats, silk stockings and gloves, net ruffles, silver buckles, and reams of velvet, lace and silk serge.[17]

The splendour and magnificence of William Brownlow's new townhouse in Dublin reflected his perceived status in Dublin society and fitted the increasing needs of his advancing political career. On 11 March 1766, even before the house was completed, he was sworn into the privy council.[18] That Brownlow opted for a French-inspired interior is not surprising. Not only was rococo very much in vogue, he also had strong personal connections with France. In 1739, at the tender age of 13, having lost in quick succession two sisters and his father, he was brought to France on doctor's orders by his mother Elizabeth Hamilton, daughter of the 6th Earl of Abercorn. He was to spend some time in France, where his widowed mother married Martin, Count de Kearny.[19] Later on as an adult he would revisit the country on several occasions. Brownlow was also sent to Italy to further his education. Between 1744 and 1748 he lived in Florence, Naples and Rome. There he took lessons and perfected harpsichord-playing skills. Music was to be an important part of Brownlow's life. He is said to have played an significant role in the creative gestation of *Midas*, a *burletta* or comic opera in the Italian fashion written by Kane O'Hara. It premiered at Crow Street Theatre in Dublin on 22 January 1762, and subsequently at the Theatre Royal, Covent Garden, London, in 1764 to great popular acclaim.[20]

William Brownlow was passionate about music, and passed this passion to his children. His daughters received a thorough education which included the learning of several musical instruments. In 1799, following the death of the youngest daughter Louisa, in Devon, aged only 17, Brownlow's widow Catherine made a claim on the estate for expenses.[21] These included not only physician's fees and medicines, but also various fees paid to a French governess, Mademoiselle Benandin, to an Italian master, a geography master and a drawing master, as well as expenses for 'musick and instruments', tambourine and piano lessons and transport of a harp.

William Brownlow's background was a learned one.[22] Both his father and grandfather had been educated at Trinity College. His grandfather Arthur Chamber-

6 – No. 12 Merrion Square: ceiling of first-floor front room
(*photo David Davison*)

lain of Niselrath, near Ardee, county Louth, adopted the surname Brownlow on inheriting the estate of his maternal grandfather Sir William Brownlow, situated in Lurgan, county Armagh. (Sir William had married Eleanor O'Dogherty of Inishowen, county Donegal.) Arthur Brownlow accumulated extensive wealth by wise management and investment.[23] His personal interest in the Irish language was widely known. He was a discerning collector of old Irish manuscripts, and also a translator. 'He took [O'Dornin] into his house to instruct his family, revise his Irish records, enrich his library with Gaelic poetry, and above all to infuse into his own

7 – No. 12 Merrion Square: detail of ceiling of first-floor front room
(photo David Davison)

mind a deep and lasting love of the literature of his native country.' [24] He was a patron of the scribe Padraig Mac Oghannan, and had in his possession the Book of Armagh (custody of which was entrusted to the Royal Irish Academy for the best part of the nineteenth century. The Book of Armagh is presently in the possession of the library of Trinity College, Dublin.) [25]

During his residence in Ireland, the celebrated American painter Gilbert Stuart (1755-1828) painted a half-length portrait of William Brownlow (*c*.1790). It shows him seated, directing a serious gaze to the spectator. He is wearing a powdered wig and holding a letter in his right hand. In spite of the formality of the portrait, the sensitive face offers a glimpse of the character of the man. Stuart was a prolific painter, and in the six years he remained in Dublin he produced a considerable number of portraits. He also painted other members of the Irish parliament: John Foster (Speaker), Henry Grattan, William Robert, Duke of Leinster, Charles Powell Leslie and Robert Shaw of Terenure.[26]

The political career of William Brownlow spanned four decades. In his last election in 1790 he published an address to the freeholders of the county of Armagh.[27] In it he exhorted his countrymen: 'Look back at my conduct and see how you have been served; for whether I have not been forward to promote every advantage that the nation has received since I have been your representative; the freeing of her constitution from the dependence in which it was so long held; shortening the duration of the parliaments, which is a proper check on the conduct of the representative; extending the freedom of trade, and encouraging the Linen in every branch; in short, everything that was done or attempted for the advantage of this country had my warmest support. However, if you are of the opinion, that you can be better served by any other man, avail yourselves of your privilege, and elect him...' He ended his address by adding: 'Let my situation in life be what it may, I shall ever remain a steady friend to my country, and never forfeit the character of an honest uncorrupt man, which I thank God I have firmly established.' That was his last election and he won it.

Brownlow's will, made in the following year and proved in November 1794, displays a sobriety and restraint quite at odds with the opulent interior of his Dublin house. In it he directed that his body be 'decently buried privately and without any ostentation or superfluous expense either in the parish where I shall die or in such other convenient place as my executors shall appoint, it being to me a matter of the utmost indifference'.[28]

———

ACKNOWLEDGEMENTS

The authors wish to thank the following individuals for their help in researching this article: the Earl of Darnley, Tom Desmond, Lord de Vesci, Clancourt Holdings, Anne Dillon, FÁS, Matthew and Patrick Forde, Patrick Fagan, Joanna Finnegan, David Griffin, Aideen Ireland, Máire Kennedy, Charles Kenny, Conor Kenny, Jeremy Rex-Parkes, Richard Wingfield. Special thanks for their help and hospitality to Mr and Mrs Jamie Brownlow.

ENDNOTES

[1] E.M. Johnston-Liik, *History of the Irish Parliament 1692-1800*, 6 vols (Belfast 2002) iii, 294.

[2] Charlemont to Dr Haliday, 20 October 1794, in Francis Hardy, *Memoirs of the Political and Private Life of James Caulfield Earl of Charlemont* (London 1810) 370.

[3] John and Edward Lees, 'Handel in Dublin', *Dublin Historical Record*, xiii, 1953, 3-4, 75. This seems unlikely as Brownlow was only 13 years old. However, a contemporary portrait with his parents (Lurgan House) depicts the young teenager playing the harpsichord.

[4] Elizabeth married 1791 John, 4th Earl Darnley; Isabella married 1796 Richard, 4th Viscount Powerscourt; Francis Laetitia married 1796 John, 2nd Viscount de Vesci (source: *Burke's Peerage and Baronetage*)

[5] Public Records Office, Northern Ireland, Brownlow Papers, D1928.

[6] PRONI, Brownlow Papers, D1928/4/3.

[7] National Archives, Dublin, Pembroke Papers 97/46/2/39.

[8] National Archives, Dublin, Pembroke Papers 97/46/1/2/6/70.

[9] Information courtesy of David Griffin.

[10] PRONI, Brownlow Papers, D1928/H/1.

[11] In this regard it is perhaps worth noting that in 1777 a James Byrne of Loughlinbridge married Catherine Archdall of Mount Eccles and built a number of houses on Great Denmark Street adjacent to Belvedere House, which was designed by West.

[12] Christine Casey, 'Boiseries, bankers and bills: a tale of Charlemont and Whaley' in Michael McCarthy (ed.), *Lord Charlemont and his circle* (Dublin 2001) 47-59.

[13] PRONI, Brownlow Papers, D1928/H/2.

[14] Armagh Museum, Patterson MSS; National Library of Ireland microfilm pos. 208.

[15] The Knight of Glin, 'A directory of the Dublin furnishing trade 1752-1800', in Agnes Bernelle (ed.), *Decantations: a tribute to Maurice Craig* (Dublin 1992) 47, 54.

[16] PRONI, Brownlow Papers, D1928/H/3.

[17] PRONI, Brownlow Papers, D1928/A/2/3.

[18] Armagh Museum, Patterson MSS; NLI microfilm pos. 208.

[19] Richard Hayes, *Biographical dictionary of Irishmen in France* (Dublin 1949) 136.

[20] Charlemont to Dr Haliday, 20 October 1794, '...he had many accomplishments; music he understood accurately, and the agreeable opera of Midas was, in some measure, planned, the airs rehearsed, and altogether prepared for the stage, at his house', in Hardy, *Memoirs*, 370.

[21] NLI, De Vesci Papers, L/3. Claim made by Catherine Brownlow, widow of W.B., to the Brownlow estate for expenses incurred relating to her daughter Louisa Brownlow.

[22] *Alumni Dublinenses, A register of the students, graduates, professors and provosts of Trinity College in the University of Dublin* (Dublin 1935) 106, 144.

[23] R.G. Gillespie, *Settlement and Survival on an Ulster Estate: the Brownlow Leasbook 1667-1771* (Belfast, 1988)

[24] J.B.L, 'Arthur Brownlow and his MSS', *The Irish Book Lover*, March-April, 1936, 26-8.

[25] Royal Irish Academy minutes, vol 2, January 1827 – March 1849, 424.

[26] L. Park, *Gilbert Stuart, an illustrated descriptive list of his works*, 1 (New York 1926) 183-4

[27] NLI, De Vesci Papers, *The Freeholders of the County of Armagh*, 17 April 1790.

[28] PRONI, Brownlow Papers, D1928/T/315

1 – Interior of the Honan Chapel, Cork, looking east
(all photos by the author)

The Honan Chapel, Cork:
a shrine to the
Irish arts and crafts movement

PAUL LARMOUR

In THE HISTORY OF THE IRISH ARTS AND CRAFTS MOVEMENT, ONE BUILDING STANDS out for its unique fusion of architecture and the decorative arts, the result of a highly successful collaboration between patron, architect, artist and craftsman.[1] That is the Honan Chapel in Cork in which various preoccupations of the Irish Revival – the Celtic Revival in art,[2] the Hiberno-Romanesque revival in architecture, and a committed interest in the use of native materials – were combined to great effect (Plate 1). In a book published at the time of its opening in 1916, the building and its furnishings were described in some detail and the genesis of its design revealed, in what was clearly a hope that the example would be followed by others.[3] It is a story worth retelling, especially as the success of the Honan Chapel was not repeated elsewhere, and its valuable collection of the best Irish ecclesiastical art of the early twentieth century was to remain unique.[4]

The Honan Chapel was the conception of Sir John Robert O'Connell, a Dublin solicitor who was legal trustee of the Honan family bequest.[5] The Honan family, who had been active in the commercial life of Cork since the late eighteenth century, had established links with University College Cork in 1909 through the creation of the Honan scholarships. With the death in 1913 of Isabella, the last member of the family, O'Connell, who as executor under her will had power to distribute a portion of the estate for charitable and educational purposes, decided to offer up to £40,000 for the benefit of the college.[6] Part of it was used to acquire a building for use as a residential hall for male students at the college, to be known as the Honan Hostel, and the rest of the money went towards building a chapel for Roman Catholic worship in association with the hostel.

O'Connell's prime motivation in building a chapel was his conviction that a university was not complete without one. There was no chapel in University College Cork, as by university statute it was a secular college. By building a chapel, ostensibly for the use of the hostel residents, O'Connell was able to make good this deficiency, as the chapel would also provide an easily accessible and convenient place of worship for the majority of students, being sited, along with the hostel, immediately adjacent to the original college buildings. In this he had the support of the college president, Sir Bertram Windle, who for some years past had wanted to secure a church in the locality where the Roman Catholic undergraduates could worship as a corporate body.[7] Having, thus, a clear conviction that a chapel should be built, O'Connell also had an equally clear vision of what form it should take.

In 'Some thoughts on church building', the opening chapter to his book on the chapel, O'Connell set out what he believed were some of the elementary principles involved in building a church, expressing his belief that it should be constructed of native and local materials, well wrought and plain, but good; that ornament should be sparingly used, and that where used it should be above reproach and display some quality worth looking at. In coming to these views he appears to have been influenced by Robert Elliott, a Dublin painter-turned-art-critic.[8] Elliott had written a number of articles critical of all branches of ecclesiastical art in Ireland, including architecture, which were published in both the Catholic and the nationalist press some years before, and had been gathered into a book titled *Art and Ireland*, published in Dublin in 1906. Elliott had been very critical of some Irish work of the recent past, for its inefficient waste, its vulgar ostentation, its monotonous use of cheap ornamentation, and its inappropriate styling, propounding instead an 'arts and crafts' philosophy of simplicity and fitness for purpose, ultimately derived from such figures in England as Pugin and Ruskin. It was this 'arts and crafts' philosophy which had clearly shaped O'Connell's thinking on the character and quality of chapel that was required.

As regards the specific form his chapel should take, O'Connell had a vision that was as clear as his general principles: 'This chapel must call into life again the spirit and work of the age when Irishmen built churches and nobly adorned them under an impulse of native genius.'[9] For him this meant a necessity to 'be faithful to those early Celtic forms to be found in so many places in this country, which for want of a better term, are known as Hiberno-Romanesque'.[10]

In his conviction that only the Hiberno-Romanesque (or Irish Romanesque) style would serve his purposes, O'Connell was following in the wake of a number of architects and patrons who had turned to the early Irish style to impart an especially native image to their buildings, from as early as the late eighteenth century, but particularly around the turn of the twentieth century. Indeed, the heyday of the revival of early Irish forms of architecture had already seen such examples in county Cork as the little oratory chapel at St Finbarre's Retreat, Gouganne Barra of 1900, and Timoleague Roman Catholic church of 1906, and, elsewhere in Munster, the Roman Catholic church at Quilty in county Clare of 1909.[11] In the second chapter of his book, O'Connell outlined the origin and development of the Hiberno-

Romanesque style, building up a case for its credentials as a distinctly 'national' style in Ireland. In reality, his chosen form of Romanesque was no more distinctively native than a number of other styles which had appeared in Ireland, as the *Irish Builder and Engineer* observed:

> It is not clear why many writers rather gratuitously assume that because a well-developed Romanesque once flourished in Ireland, that therefore no other style was rooted in the country, whereas the sequence of styles followed pretty much the same course here as in other countries. Indeed, in this particular instance there is room for argument whether the more appropriate style would not have been some form or development of that much neglected, but characteristic phase, late Irish Gothic, in view of the architectural character of the surrounding college buildings.[12]

The Hiberno-Romanesque style of architecture preferred by O'Connell, however, held the popular nationalist appeal of conjuring up a vision of a supposed golden age from the past, and certainly it did relate to a particularly splendid period of art in Ireland. Thus, against a background of 'arts and crafts' ideology and romantic nationalist Celtic Revivalism, O'Connell not only decided to build the chapel in the Irish Romanesque style of architecture, but also to have all its fittings and furnishings 'designed and fashioned for it as parts of a thought-out scheme', an effort to make it 'an expression of the best work which can be produced in Ireland today'.[13] Among those to be recruited to the task were some of the leading figures in the Irish arts and crafts movement.

In the spirit of Irish Revivalism of the time, O'Connell was also keen to emphasise not only the national qualities of the architecture and its fittings and furnishings, but also its local character and relevance. The chapel was to be dedicated to St Finn Barr because it would stand on a site which was probably part of his original monastery. It would pay tribute to a number of other local saints in some of its decorative elements, while many of the artists, craftworkers and other personnel who were to be employed on it would come from Cork, and the main building material was also to be local.[14]

The chapel was designed in 1914, the foundation stone laid on 18 May 1915, and the building was completed in 1916, the official opening being on 5 November, although the last windows were not actually fitted until early 1917.[15] The architect was James F. McMullen of Cork, and the builders were John Sisk & Son of Cork. McMullen was a well-known public figure, having been High Sheriff for the City of Cork in 1907-08, and a prominent enough architect, having been involved in hospital and office design, but he appears to have had no special experience in ecclesiastical architecture; it may be assumed that his role was little more than that of

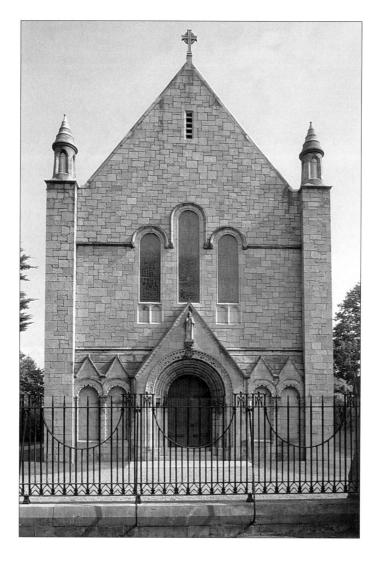

2 – The Honan Chapel: west front

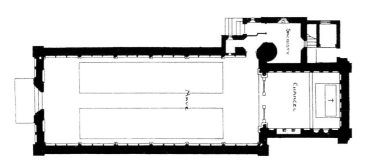

3 – The Honan Chapel: ground-floor plan
(*from* THE HONAN HOSTEL CHAPEL, CORK, *1916*)

executant architect required to give substance to O'Connell's already well-developed ideas and bring them to reality.[16] Between the two of them, architect and patron, the Honan Chapel took shape.

The result of O'Connell and McMullen's collaboration was a building essentially in Hiberno-Romanesque style, in which a number of important early Irish churches were quoted, but the treatment was very free. There were a number of elements that were not archaeologically correct in relation to O'Connell's original vision, but the particular selection of details was skilfully welded together to create a fairly satisfying whole.

In plan the building comprises a long nave and a deep square-ended chancel, with a small sacristy on the north side and a small circular belfry rising from it (Plate 3). It thus followed the typical Irish Romanesque 'nave and chancel' type of plan of the twelfth century as found at the likes of Kilmalkedar in county Kerry. Built of white Cork limestone, the walls externally were faced with punched ashlar, mostly in random courses of squared rubble, but with some parts, such as the belfry, executed in coursed ashlar. In character the architectural treatment of the building was generally plain, relieved only by a corbel course to each side and chevron carvings to the west front arches, with ornamental elements confined to small carved label stops to windows and some more elaborate carved work at the western entrance.

The overall design of the west gable (Plate 2) was based on that of St Cronan's church at Roscrea, county Tipperary, as O'Connell acknowledged in his book.[17] It provided the model for an arcaded treatment of the west wall, with what are termed 'tangent' gables over both the central entrance and the flanking arcades, and what appear to be 'antae' at the extremities of the gable. The church at Roscrea also gave the idea for the inclusion of a sculpted figure in the gablet over the doorway of the new chapel. In the place of St Cronan at Roscrea we find St Finn Barr here at Cork, garbed in the raiment of a bishop, with Celtic interlacements decorating the vestment and the ornamented corbel on which the figure stands (Plate 4). The figure was carved by Oliver Sheppard (1865-1941), Professor of Sculpture at the Dublin School of Art and the leading sculptor in Ireland at the time.

To each side of the main doorway the capitals of the columns are sculpted as human heads, representing six well-known Munster saints: Colman, patron saint of Cloyne, Gobnait of Ballyvourney, Declan of Ardmore, Finn Barr of Cork, Ita of Limerick, and Brendan of Kerry. With their intertwining locks, they appear to have been based on the carved doorway capitals at the old Romanesque church at Killeshin in county Laois, and were carved by Henry Emery of Dublin, assisted by a band of young stone-carving apprentices selected by him from the Cork Technical School. The doors themselves, constructed of oak, are hung from large wrought iron

4 – Statue of St Finn Barr by Oliver Sheppard (1865-1941) over the west doorway

opposite

5 – View of the Honan Chapel from the north-east

strapwork hinges of a Celticised Art Nouveau pattern, made by the metalworkers J. and C. McGloughlin, of Dublin, and almost certainly designed by William A. Scott (1871-1921), Professor of Architecture at University College Dublin.[18] Scott had been commissioned to design a fine pair of wrought iron grille gates in a very freely treated Celtic style with interlaced panels and spiralled bosses, and incorporating a full-width Celtic cross motif. Hand-hammered by McGloughlin's, the grille gates were originally mounted in the doorway immediately across the face of the doors, and permitted a view of the interior through the open doors while keeping the chapel locked, but they have now been removed.[19]

Elsewhere on the exterior, the position of the belfry, in the angle between nave and chancel, and its form, a miniature Irish round tower, was clearly influenced by Temple Finghin at Clonmacnoise, county Offaly, an Irish Romanesque ruin of the twelfth century, while the small circular window, decorated by chevrons in the apex of the east gable, was presumably inspired by the restored remains of a twelfth century Irish Romanesque church at Freshford in county Kilkenny.

Notwithstanding the academic authority that its range of historical quotations seems to suggest, the building is not consistent in its adherence to Irish Romanesque precedent. The roof pitch is not quite steep enough to be archaeologically convincing, and the 'antae' at the west end are more in the form of clasping buttresses than

simple projections of the side walls beyond the gable, as found in genuine Irish
early Christian and Romanesque buildings. The little angle turrets on the west front,
in the form of conically capped arcaded drums of stone, are also not characteristic
of the Irish Romanesque style, but they do respond here to a theme suggested by the
gate piers at the front and expressed more fully elsewhere on the building, that is, in
the belfry at the north-east corner. The form of the buttresses at the east gable also
suggests a Gothic rather than a Romanesque model, and from a strictly archaeological point of view are therefore unsatisfactory. Otherwise the building is pleasing in
its mass and compositional arrangement outside, not least when viewed from the
north-east (Plate 5).

The main west doorway leads to a lofty interior laid out as a simple nave and
chancel, its barrel-vaulted form of roof with transverse ribs, prominent chancel arch,
and arcading to the side walls all inspired by Cormac's Chapel, the celebrated
twelfth-century Romanesque church at Cashel, but whereas Cormac's Chapel is all
of stonework, the ceiling here is of plaster and its transverse ribs are of timber (Plate
1). The arcading and other dressings of the walls are of the same fine grey Cork
limestone as used on the exterior, set against plain white plaster, with the capitals to
the nave arcade columns all carved differently and featuring birds and animals
among the range of motifs. This arcading in the nave forms a framework to the sta-

tions of the cross made of *opus sectile*, literally 'cut work' of richly coloured glass embedded in the plasterwork of the wall, in the middle of each triple-arched bay (Plate 6). O'Connell was keen on this method of creating stations as it was a more permanent alternative to the conventional paintings that were usually used in Irish churches and often ended up hung or knocked askew, thus causing irritation to the more aesthetically minded worshippers. The method had been employed in Ireland as early as 1908 by Sarah Purser's studio, An Túr Gloine, or 'The Tower of Glass', who were actually working on a set of similar stations for Spiddal church in county Galway during 1916, but O'Connell seems to have been unaware of the fact that *opus sectile* could be made in Ireland, and went elsewhere with the commission for the Honan.[20] It was carried out for him by the firm of L. Oppenheimer Ltd, based in Manchester, and was one of only two elements within the chapel that were not executed by Irish firms; the other was the mosaic flooring, also carried out by Oppenheimer, although their role has never been publicised.[21] Although he enthused about the floor itself, O'Connell did not identify the firm responsible in his book in 1916, presumably because such recourse to an outside firm would not have been seen to be consistent with the aim to foster Irish arts and crafts.

Presumably as a result of O'Connell's reticence on the matter, other contemporary references also fail to identify the firm responsible for the mosaic work, and

6 – A 'station of the cross' by L. Oppenheimer Ltd

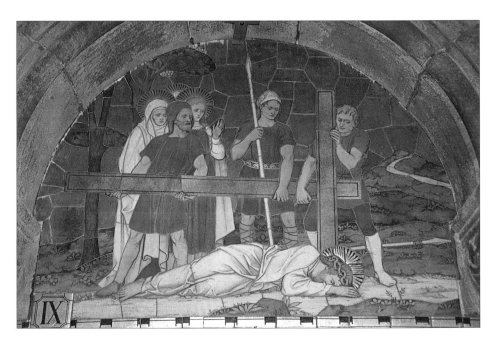

so, remarkably, the actual designer of the floor remains anonymous.[22] This is unfortunate as the floor is the most spectacular thing of its type in Ireland.[23] The entire scheme, covering both the nave and the chancel, dwells on 'the Creation and the works of the Lord'. On entering the chapel by the west door, one first sees a large circular panel at the west end depicting the sun, surrounded by signs of the zodiac, in roundels linked by zoomorphic Celtic interlace, with trees, plants and animals to each side (Plate 16). The central aisle depicts the 'river of life', containing fish and other creatures, flowing eastward, and at the east end of the nave in front of the chancel is a design depicting animals, birds, fish and trees, representing 'the work of God's Hands' (Plate 14). In the chancel itself is a multi-circled design showing such things as the sun and moon, stars and planets, wind and snow, rain and ice, trees and fruit, and birds and fish, arranged around a central circular panel depicting the earth. The entire floor of the nave and chancel, except for pewed areas and the sanctuary dais, comprises very colourful mosaic designs, vigorously drawn, and bordered with Celtic interlaced and zoomorphic ornament (Plate 15).

Originally the chancel was marked off from the nave by low arcaded communion rails of cut limestone, in the centre of which was an opening without a gate, but these rails have now been removed. The arcaded lower walls of the chancel differ somewhat from those of the nave, being more elaborately ornamented with chevron or zigzag carvings to the arches, and the pilasters have been cut with lozenge patterning directly inspired by nave arcading at Cormac's Chapel. There is also a small aumbry or recess on the south side, taking the place of a credence table, with a triple-arched sedilia, or seating recess, adjacent to it.

The altar consists of a large slab of limestone carved with a frieze of chevron ornament, resting on five rectangular piers which have each face carved with a different pattern of Irish cross, and on the slab or table itself stands the tabernacle which forms the focal point of the whole building (Plate 13). Constructed of limestone, the tabernacle takes the form of an early Irish oratory with a steeply pitched roof, its surfaces to the sides carved in relief with panels of Celtic ornamentation, while its front face contains a door and tympanum in coloured enamel designed and made by Oswald Reeves (1870-1967). Reeves was a talented graphic artist and a master of enamelled metalwork, which he taught at the Dublin School of Art.[24] The door panel depicts the Adoration of the Lamb, with the 'tree of life' and groups of angels bearing the implements of crucifixion, while the triangular panel over the door represents the Blessed Trinity, with attendant angels bearing in their arms the sun and the moon as symbols of 'the days of Creation' (Plate 9). Together they comprise a splendid conception carried out in brilliant and luminous enamels on repoussé silver, partially guilded, and set in a bronze surround – 'the finest thing of its kind in Ireland', adjudged the *Irish Builder* some years later.[25]

The chancel was provided with hangings made by the Dun Emer Guild, of Dublin, comprising an embroidered antependium designed by Katherine MacCormack (1892-1975) for the front of the altar, and a magnificent tapestry dossal which covers the lower part of the east wall.[26] The antependium represents in the centre the figure of Christ seated and encircled by a frame, flanked immediately to the left by St Patrick and St Columcille, and to the right by St Brigid and St Finn Barr, with kneeling figures of St Ita and St Colman occupying the outer panels. The groundwork is of dull gold, all worked over on canvas, on which the various figures and symbols were raised in silk thread of various rich colours.

The dossal is a splendid piece, of rich red colour divided into four panels, on each of which have been woven symbols of the four evangelists derived from examples in the Book of Kells, and rich borders of early Irish geometrical ornament. It was designed by Katherine MacCormack jointly with her aunt Evelyn Gleeson (1855-1944), the foundress of the Dun Emer Guild. The guild also provided specially woven hand-tufted carpets for the chancel, in which early Irish geometrical patterns were used for the borders, thus relating them to both the dossal and the antependium, an embroidered cope,[27] and an embroidered banner depicting St Finn Barr, with Celtic interlaced borders. Such richly worked textiles were calculated to give warmth and glowing colour to an otherwise austere and sombre interior (Plate 7).

The Celtic theme apparent in so much of the chapel's ornamentation was taken up very effectively in the splendid vestments, made of Irish poplin, and embroidered by a team of about thirty girls over a period of eighteen months in the workshop of William Egan & Sons in Cork.[28] The 'cloth of gold' set consisting of a cope, chasuble and dalmatic for High Mass, together with associated stoles and veils, was designed by Ethel Josephine Scally of Cork, who died in July 1915 before the work was completed.[29] The work for that set took nearly twelve months to make, the designs comprising medallions of the four evangelists, taken from the Book of Kells, set in bands of freely intertwining serpentine ornament. The other sets of vestments – red, white, violet, green and black, along with some miscellaneous examples in purple – were designed by John Lees of Cork.[30] They are covered with vigorous but well-controlled phytomorphic interlace designs carried out in richly coloured threads (Plate 8). Shields bearing the arms of the Honan hostel were incorporated on a number of the vestments, about which Sir John O'Connell wrote:

I am very happy to think that the making of these elaborate and beautiful sets

_____

7 – View of the sanctuary showing dossal, antependium, and carpets, all designed and made by the Dun Emer Guild

8 – Embroidered vestment, designed by John Lees and made by William Egan & Sons

9 – Tabernacle enamels by Oswald Reeves

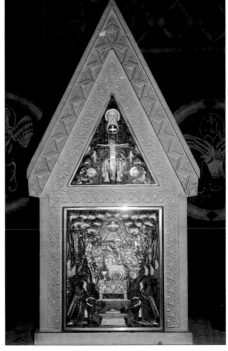

10, 11, 12 – Censer, sanctuary lamp and monstrance, designed by William A. Scott,
made by Edmond Johnson Ltd

13 – View of the sanctuary with altar and east wall uncovered

of vestments has given a lengthened period of much-needed employment to a considerable number of young women, who have shown much interest and acquired a high degree of technical skill in carrying to perfection these beautiful designs.[31]

Several of the embroideresses' names were recorded on the inside of some of the vestments.[32]

The firm of William Egan & Sons also made a chalice and ciborium for the chapel, both in silver-gilt, decorated with bands of Celtic interlace. Most of the altar plate, however, was made by the firm of Edmond Johnson of Dublin, most notably a set which was designed by Professor William A. Scott, the Dublin architect. It comprises a crucifix, six altar candlesticks, and a missal stand, all in brass, an incense boat, a censer (Plate 10), a pair of cruets, and a monstrance, all in silver-gilt, and a sanctuary lamp in silver (Plate 11). The sanctuary lamp bears a quaint neomedievalising inscription, part of which reads 'Sir John Robert O'Connell Doctor of Laws ordered me to be made, William Alphonsus Scott first Professor of Architecture of the National University of Ireland designed me, Edmond Johnson of Dublin fashioned me AD1916'. All of the pieces in the set by Scott display his per-

16 – Detail of nave floor by L. Oppenheimer Ltd

opposite 14, 15 – Details of nave floor and chancel floor by L. Oppenheimer Ltd

sonal rendering of freely treated Celtic ornament, and show him to have been an inventive designer of rare individuality who could adapt and extend a comparatively limited historic convention well beyond the normal range of its applications. A particularly outstanding piece is the monstrance, a highly original conception, the design around the head symbolising a flight of doves treated freely in Celtic fashion (Plate 12).

Apart from the pieces designed by Scott, the firm of Edmond Johnson also provided other items, such as a ciborium and a chalice in silver-gilt, which were more conventional in their use of Celtic ornament, as well as a large processional cross in silver with semi-precious stones and enamel bosses, virtually a reproduction, in restored form, of the Cross of Cong, one of the most intricately ornamented examples of early Irish art.

In every detail the furnishing of the chapel was carefully considered. Eleanor Kelly of Dublin was responsible for the tooled bindings of the missals, including a 'Mass book of the dead' [33] for the commemoration of the chapel's founders, the design on the front cover of which was copied from the old Irish cross slab at Tullylease in county Cork. Another Dublin artist, Joseph Tierney, designed and illuminated a set of altar cards which are beautifully lettered and ornamented with colourful and very intricate Celtic designs. They were mounted in bejew-

17 – Altar card designed by Joseph Tierney, with frame executed by Edmond Johnson Ltd
18 – Carved oak pews, made by J. Sisk & Son

elled and enamelled silver frames made by Edmond Johnson's firm (Plate 17). Even the oak pews were specially designed in accord with the Hiberno-Romanesque and Celtic theme, with chevron ornamentation on the ends of the pews and on a pair of ceremonial chairs, with panels of pierced interlace on their associated kneelers (Plate 18). The oak furnishings were made by the builders Sisk & Son, presumably to designs by the architect James McMullen.

The chief glory of the interior, however, is the stained glass, all of it Irish. Eight of the nineteen lights were by members of Sarah Purser's well-established Dublin studio, An Túr Gloine,[34] and the remaining eleven were by the new young Dublin artist, Harry Clarke (1889-1931).[35] Initially O'Connell had approached Sarah Purser (1848-1943) with a commission for some windows at the chapel, and Purser, understandably enough, had formed the impression that her studio, which enjoyed a position of pre-eminence in Ireland, would do all of them,[36] but O'Connell's attention had also been drawn to the emerging artist Harry Clarke, and he had invited him to submit some designs. O'Connell was so impressed with the result that he extended the original order to Clarke until eventually his contribution outnumbered that of An Túr Gloine.

The windows comprise, in the chancel, the east window of Our Lord by Alfred Child (1875-1939), scenes from the Gospel of St John by Catherine O'Brien (1882-1963) in the north wall, and windows of Our Lady and of St Joseph in the south wall, both by Harry Clarke. In the nave is a series of windows depicting the patron saints of the dioceses which make up the province of Munster, and other saints closely bound up with Cork. These are Finn Barr, Albert, Declan, Ita, Brendan and Gobnait by Clarke; Ailbe, Fachtna and Colman by Child; Munchin and Flannan by O'Brien; and Cathage by Ethel Rhind (1877-1952). At the west end appear the 'Trias Thaumaturga', the three wonder-working saints of Ireland, Patrick, Brigid and Columcille, all by Clarke.

There is a great difference in style between the works of the two studios. The windows by Clarke are a blaze of rich, deep colours, and contain stylised figures in brilliant garments and bejewelled settings. Those by Purser's studio are, on the whole, characterised by the use of paler tints and by more naturalistic presentation of the human form.

Two of the windows by An Túr Gloine, those of St Ailbe (Plate 22) and St Colman, by Child, incorporate representations of architectural canopies of Romanesque type, with Celtic interlaced ornamentation to the borders and other elements, thereby conforming very overtly to the overall stylistic theme of the chapel's architecture, whereas the windows of St Flannan and St Munchin (Plate 23) by O'Brien, and St Carthage by Rhind, eschew conventional canopy-work for more closely integrated subsidiary scenes to both top and bottom. Together with the well-

19, 20, 21 – Details of the St Albert, St Declan and St Gobnait windows by Harry Clarke

considered iconography, which features crosses and croziers of Irish type, these illustrations of incidents from the saints' lives add interest to each composition.

The windows by Clarke, being the work of one individual, are more consistent in their treatment. Each one depicts a full-length figure surrounded by a wealth of symbolic and iconographical detail, exquisitely drawn and glowing with brilliant colour. Saints Patrick, Brigid and Columcille are fine harmonies in blues and greens, their rich and solemn colours blended with taste and skill. St Finn Barr is robed in a chasuble of rich red colour, and St Ita is garbed in deep royal blue, all of them set in a rich tapestry of symbolic emblems and names in Irish script, interspersed with scenes from their lives.

The St Albert window depicts the saint sitting enthroned, staring straight ahead and raising a green silk-gloved hand in blessing, above chequer-work detailed figures, with a crucifix behind him which bears the face of the artist himself (Plate 19), while the St Brendan window shows its subject standing imperiously, surround-

ed by borders of richly plumed birds, recalling one of the legends associated with him. The St Declan window stands out as a particularly jewel-like achievement of kaleidoscopic richness, in which the yellow-garbed saint stands above Celtic-spi-ralled waves, and holds in one hand a model of Ardmore Cathedral and round tower, and in the other a Celtic ornamented silver staff (Plate 20). The St Gobnait window is yet another brilliant example of its artist's inventive approach, with a decorative use of a honeycomb pattern – Gobnait being the patroness of bees – and her nimbus given the shape of a stone cross which was at one time associated with her cult (Plate 21). Meanwhile, in the two Clarke windows not representing Irish saints, those of Our Lady and of St Joseph, the subjects are drawn into the overall scheme by the incorporation of Celtic interlace at their feet.

The overall effect of Clarke's windows is a richly decorative one, in the manner of the best medieval glass. The amount of original and sometimes fantastic detail is astounding, whilst the depth of brilliance of colours is breathtaking. It was a remarkable achievement for a young man still in his twenties, and critics and connoisseurs were full of praise for Clarke's windows.[37] As Thomas Bodkin wrote at the time, 'Nothing like them has been produced before in Ireland. The sustained magnificence of colour, the beautiful and most intricate drawings, the lavish and mysterious symbolism, combine to produce an effect of splendour which is over-powering.'[38]

Meanwhile, Clarke's fellow artist at the Honan Chapel, Oswald Reeves, enthusiastically wrote of his contribution:

These windows reveal a conception of stained glass that stands quite alone ... There has never been before such mastery of technique, nor such application of it to the ends of exceeding beauty, significance, and wondrousness. No one has ever before shown the great beauty that can be obtained by the leads alone, nor the mysterious beauty and 'liveness' that each piece of glass receives at the hand of this artist, nor the jewelled gorgeousness of 'pattern' that may be given to a window that teems with subject interest and meaning.[39]

Although the stained glass in the Honan Chapel was the work of different artists, and the design and technique differed, the overall result is nonetheless harmonious. There is an intrinsic artistic quality to each of the individual windows, whether by Clarke or by the Purser studio, and there is what looks like a fair degree of co-ordination of subject and treatment. All but one of the windows is a single-figure subject, with the scale of the figures reasonable in proportion to the overall size of the window, while the subsidiary subjects are not inharmonious in scale or treatment. The glass thus rendered the Honan Chapel not just remarkable amongst contemporary churches in Ireland, but of considerable interest in a wider context, as the *Irish*

Builder acknowledged:

> No other building of its size that we know of, possesses so complete and har-
> monious a series of modern glass of equal quality. Instances like Mr
> Christopher Whall's splendid glass at Gloucester Cathedral, the Burne Jones
> windows at Birmingham Cathedral, the works of the late Mr Charles Kempe
> and the many younger artists in England, of course, recur to mind, and in
> Ireland the chancel lights of Loughrea Cathedral, as well as other examples;
> but these are all in either much larger and more important structures, or else
> specimens interspersed amongst other glass. Cork is to be congratulated upon
> its acquisition of a unique collection of modern glass.[40]

Not alone the glass, of course, but all the furnishings and fittings of the Honan
Chapel together contributed to what would turn out to be a unique record of the best
Irish ecclesiastical art of the time. Its creator Sir John O'Connell had expressed the
hope in 1916 that by its example 'the standard of perfection of design and art work
in church building in Ireland may be corrected and improved',[41] while the *Irish
Builder* shortly afterwards held it up as 'a very valuable and much-needed object
lesson to those possessing patronage, and to the Irish public generally'.[42]

Although there were to be further instances in Ireland of enlightened patronage leading to some very fine examples of Irish ecclesiastical art in the decades that
followed, the special achievement at the Honan Chapel was never repeated. The
conditions that had led to its particularly successful collaboration of patron, architect, artist and craftsman, all working together to a common purpose, did not occur
again, having not only arisen from the particular artistic values and cultural milieu
that pertained at the time, but also having depended on a very personal visionary
zeal, allied to what appear to have been plentiful funds. The Honan Chapel thus represents a unique achievement. In its characteristically Irish architectural form, combined with the largely Celtic ornamentalist manner of much of its furnishings, and
its overriding preoccupation with unity of artistic expression and purpose, and high-
quality craftsmanship, it stands today as both a remarkable expression of the Celtic
Revival and a shrine to the Irish arts and crafts movement.[43]

———

ACKNOWLEDGMENTS

The author wishes to thank successive chaplains and wardens in charge of the Honan Hostel
Chapel for access to its collection at various times from 1974 to 1991 for the purposes of photog-
raphy, particularly Rev Michael Crowley and Prof Finbarr Holland, and also to thank the trustees
for permission to reproduce the photographs.

22 – *St Ailbe window*
by Alfred Child of An Túr Gloine

23 – *St Munchin window*
by Catherine O'Brien of An Túr Gloine

ENDNOTES

[1] See P. Larmour, *The Arts and Crafts Movement in Ireland* (Belfast 1992); and P. Larmour, 'Arts and Crafts Movement', in B. de Breffny (ed.), *Ireland: A Cultural Encyclopaedia* (London 1983) 36.

[2] See P. Larmour, *Celtic Ornament*, Irish Heritage Series, 33 (Dublin 1981); and P. Larmour, 'Celtic Revival', in de Breffny (ed.), *Ireland: A Cultural Encyclopaedia*, 58-9

[3] Sir John R. O'Connell, *The Honan Hostel Chapel, Cork: Some notes on the building and the ideals which inspired it* (Cork 1916).

[4] Descriptions of the building and its contents subsequent to O'Connell's account in 1916 include the following: *The Irish Builder and Engineer*, 31 March 1917, 150-2, 154; 28 April 1917, 198-200, 202; Rev Sir John R. O'Connell, *The Collegiate Chapel, Cork* (Cork 1932); M.J. O'Kelly, 'The Honan Chapel', *The Furrow*, vol 1, no 6, July 1950, 290-6; M.J. O'Kelly, *The Honan Chapel* (Cork 1966); P. Larmour, 'The Celtic Revival and a National Style of Architecture', unpublished PhD thesis, Queen's University of Belfast, 1977; N. Gordon Bowe, 'A Host of Shining Saints: Harry Clarke's Stained Glass in Cork', *Country Life*, clxvi, no. 4279, 12 July 1979, 114, 117; J. Sheehy, *The Rediscovery of Ireland's Past: The Celtic Revival 1830-1930* (London 1980) 118, 135-6, 142 et seq; N. Gordon Bowe, 'Honan Chapel', in de Breffny (ed.), *Ireland: A Cultural Encyclopaedia*, 108; Larmour, *The Arts and Crafts Movement in Ireland*, 84, 133-6, 160 et seq; E.W. Heckett and C.V. Teehan, *Treasures from the Honan Chapel*, exhibition catalogue (Cork 1995); P. Larmour, 'Honan Hostel Chapel', in A. Becker, J. Olley, W. Wang (eds), *20th-Century Architecture: Ireland* (Munich & New York 1997) 100-01.

[5] Sir John Robert O'Connell (1868-1943) was knighted in 1914 and was ordained a priest in 1929. For further biographical details and portrait photograph, see W.T. Pike (ed.), *Dublin and County in the Twentieth Century: Contemporary Biographies* (Brighton & London 1908) 182; and *Who Was Who, Vol IV, 1941-1950* (London 1952) 861. Following the success of the Honan Chapel he was elected to the council of the Arts and Crafts Society of Ireland in February 1917, and wrote the foreword to the catalogue of the Society's exhibition that year.

[6] As recounted in Monica Taylor, *Sir Bertram Windle: A Memoir* (London 1932) 226.

[7] *ibid.*, 228.

[8] In the revised edition of his book, published in 1932, O'Connell quoted passages from Elliott's writings at pages 11, 18-19.

[9] O'Connell, *The Honan Hostel Chapel*, 11.

[10] *ibid.*, 21.

[11] For the development of Hiberno-Romanesque Revival architecture, see Larmour, 'The Celtic Revival and a National Style of Architecture'. See also Sheehy, *The Rediscovery of Ireland's Past*.

[12] *The Irish Builder and Engineer*, 31 March 1917, 150.

[13] O'Connell, *The Honan Hostel Chapel*, 55.

[14] Significantly, Sir Bertram Windle, president of University College Cork, was a keen advocate of Irish industrial development (it was, for instance, his idea to have an Irish National Trade Mark in 1906), and he had also supported Irish arts and crafts having commissioned the Celtic ornamented mace made for University College Cork in 1910.

[15] Contemporary references to the building at various stages are found in: *The Irish Builder and*

Engineer, 5 December 1914, 665 (contract secured by Sisk); 28 October 1916, 529 (chapel almost complete); *The Cork Examiner*, 23 October 1916, 4 (description of the building); 6 November 1916, 6 (report on opening); 7 November 1916, 3 (description of monstrance).

[16] For biographical details of McMullen, with a portrait photograph, see W.T. Pike (ed.), *Cork and County in the Twentieth Century: Contemporary Biographies* (Brighton 1911) 243.

[17] O'Connell, *The Honan Hostel Chapel*, 31. The Roscrea front had previously been used as the model for the façade of Rathdaire Memorial Church of Ireland church, Ballybrittas, county Laois, in 1887 by the architect James Franklin Fuller.

[18] For Scott, see P. Larmour, 'The Drunken Man of Genius: William A. Scott (1871-1921)', *Irish Architectural Review 2001*, 3 (Dublin and Cork, 2001), 28-41.

[19] The grille gates were removed sometime before 1969 and put in storage. Detail illustrated in Larmour, *Celtic Ornament*.

[20] Details of early work in *opus sectile* by An Túr Gloine are given in Larmour, *The Arts and Crafts Movement in Ireland*, 169, 225: note 50. An Túr Gloine went on to provide other sets of *opus sectile* stations of the cross at Loughrea Cathedral, county Galway, in 1929-32, and St Anthony's Roman Catholic Church, Athlone, county Westmeath, in 1934-36.

[21] The identity of the firm responsible for the floor was revealed by the late John Sisk, son of the original builder of the chapel, Richard Sisk, and grandson of the founder of their firm, in conversation with this author and Virginia Teehan.

[22] *The Cork Examiner*, 23 October 1916, 4, praised the floor but made no reference to the designer or firm responsible; *The Irish Builder and Engineer*, 28 October 1916, 529, merely stated that 'the floor is inlaid with mosaic', while the same journal's long description of the chapel in its issue of 31 March 1917 made no reference to the floor at all.

[23] Other examples of early twentieth-century Celtic-ornamented mosaic floors – such as at St Columba's RC church, Drumcondra, Dublin; the Roman Catholic cathedrals at Cobh in county Cork, Newry in county Down, and Armagh; and St Columkille's RC church, Ballyhackamore, Belfast (laid by Oppenheimer Ltd in 1928) – are either composed mainly of repetitive interlaced knotwork or are less ambitious in scope.

[24] For Reeves see P. Larmour, 'The works of Oswald Reeves (1870-1967) artist and craftsman: an interim catalogue', *Irish Architectural and Decorative Studies*, 1 (Dublin 1998), 34-59.

[25] *The Irish Builder and Engineer*, 14 June 1924. See also 13 April 1918, 189, for a report on the work when it was completed and put on view at the Metropolitan School of Art in Dublin.

[26] For the Dun Emer Guild, see P. Larmour, 'The Dun Emer Guild', *Irish Arts Review*, vol. 1, no. 4 (1984) 24-8; and Larmour, *The Arts and Crafts Movement in Ireland*, 151-62.

[27] As recorded in *The Arts and Crafts Society of Ireland catalogue of the fifth exhibition* (Dublin 1917) 43 (item 154). The Dun Emer Guild was commissioned to make a further vestment for the chapel in 1953.

[28] As recorded in a letter from O'Connell to Francis J. Bigger of Belfast on 12 November 1916. Letter inserted in the copy of O'Connell's book (1916 edition) held in the Bigger Collection, Belfast Central Library. The letter also reveals that Bigger had assisted O'Connell in the matter of the coats of arms which appeared on the windows of the patron saints and were also sculpted on the capitals nearest to those windows.

[29] Scally's death and her role as designer were recorded in an embroidered inscription inside the chasuble of the 'cloth of gold' set of vestments.

[30] Lees was not named in either edition of O'Connell's book, but his role was recorded in *The*

Studio, October 1917, 16, in which a white chasuble was illustrated, and also *The Arts and Crafts Society of Ireland catalogue of the fifth exhibition*, 42 (items 152, 153). Two chasubles (including the white one) and accessories for the Honan Chapel, to his design, were exhibited. A detail of the white stole is illustrated in Sheehy, *The Rediscovery of Ireland's Past*, 165, but the wrong designer's name is given, and similarly so for the black vestment, also designed by Lees, illustrated at page 166.

[31] O'Connell, *The Honan Hostel Chapel*, 57.

[32] They include M. Barrett, N. Ahearne, N. Harte, M. Countie, A. Calnan, K. Cramer, K. Allman, T. Good, M. Desmond, M.E. Jenkins, M. Twomey, N. Barry. Others named in *The Arts and Crafts Society of Ireland catalogue of the fifth exhibition*, 51, were M. O'Mahony, N. Spillane, N. Callanan, N. Good, K. Carter, M. Driscoll, K. Quirke, and J. De Raedt.

[33] As it was termed in *The Arts and Crafts Society of Ireland catalogue of the fifth exhibition*, 51 (item 228).

[34] For An Túr Gloine, see Larmour, *The Arts and Crafts Movement in Ireland*, 163-71.

[35] For Harry Clarke, see Larmour, *The Arts and Crafts Movement in Ireland*, 183-90; and N Gordon Bowe, *The Life and Work of Harry Clarke* (Dublin 1989).

[36] As recounted in J. White and M. Wynne, *Irish Stained Glass* (Dublin 1963) 13.

[37] See, for instance, *The Irish Builder and Engineer*, 11 March 1916. See also White and Wynne, *Irish Stained Glass* 13, for praise by Sir Bertram Windle and Professor Patrick Abercrombie.

[38] As quoted in *The Studio*, October 1917, 21.

[39] *ibid.*, 21.

[40] *The Irish Builder and Engineer*, 28 April 1917, 198.

[41] O'Connell, *The Honan Hostel Chapel*, 60.

[42] *The Irish Builder and Engineer*, 28 April 1917, 198.

[43] The Honan Chapel collection remains almost complete, although a number of items, mainly some vestments, have deteriorated due to adverse environmental storage conditions, and other items are not in current use due to changed liturgical practice. There have also been some changes which have altered the original appearance of the interior, namely the introduction of further furnishings in the 1980s and 1990s, but essentially the chapel remains intact.

1 – Lord Chancellor of Ireland's purse from the reign of George V
(courtesy Bank of Ireland)

Trappings of sovereignty: the accoutrements of the Lords Chancellor of Ireland

PATRICIA McCABE

T HE LORD CHANCELLORSHIP OF IRELAND, AN OFFICE NOW EXTINCT, WAS ONE OF legal and political importance. The post was established under British rule when, after the Anglo-Norman invasion of Ireland in 1169 and the subsequent English occupation, an English legal system gradually superseded the Irish Brehon laws.[1] As chief law officer, the Chancellor presided as supreme judge in the Court of Chancery, and in addition was chairman of the Irish House of Lords. With the title of Lord Justice, he frequently acted as temporary governor of Ireland when the chief governor (Lord Lieutenant) was absent from Dublin. In 1800, following the Act of Union, the Irish House of Lords was disbanded. The office of Lord Chancellor continued, but his official functions thereafter were mainly concerned with legal matters. Following the establishment of the Irish Free State in 1922, the authority vested in the Lord Chancellor passed to the Chief Justice.[2] An array of accoutrements associated with the office – a Great Seal and the purse in which it was carried, a mace and an official gown – were similar to those held by the Lord Chancellor of England. Ceremonial aspects of the office were also duplicated in both countries.

The Great Seal of Ireland was a verification of royal authority entrusted to the Lord Chancellor by the monarch. Royal approval was also acknowledged by the royal arms, which were central to the ornamentation of the richly embroidered purse. The gilded mace accompanied the Chancellor when he presided in the House of Lords or the Court of Chancery. A slender white wand, a signifier of augmented power, was carried before a chancellor when, as Lord Chief Steward, he presided as supreme judge in the Irish House of Lords at trials of peers.[3] The white rod was ceremoniously broken by the Clerk of the Parliaments at the close of the trial.[4] The Chancellor's black robe trimmed with gold lace also proclaimed his jurisdiction.

Hilary Jenkinson maintained that the Great Seal of Ireland was 'perhaps the most important and almost certainly the earliest of a number of Deputed or Department seals' which extended the authority of the Great Seal of England.[5]

Jenkinson also believed that the seal 'must have been in existence in 1227 when what is probably the earliest dateable copy of the Registrum Omnium Brevium was sent over to Dublin as a model for the procedure of an Irish Chancery'.[6]

Available information indicates that the Great Seal of Ireland was made in England and was, with some minor differences, a replica of the Great Seal of England. The term 'Great Seal' refers to the matrix, which consists of two circular open boxes, about six inches in diameter, made of precious metal, the inner bases of which were engraved with appropriate designs. The traditional design for Great Seals showed the sovereign enthroned on the obverse, and an equestrian image of the monarch on the reverse, but variations occurred in the artists' depictions of the themes. Gold and silver have been used to make the matrices. The present English seal consists of an alloy, mostly silver.[7]

Except when the royal arms are changed, or as in the cases of Elizabeth I and Queen Victoria, whose reigns were particularly long ones, it is customary to make only one Great Seal during a reign. The Great Seal of Ireland of the United Kingdom of Great Britain and Ireland, issued in 1801 in the aftermath of the Act of Union, was also an exception to that custom.[8]

The making of the Great Seals and other State seals, which had been 'jobbed out to all and sundry', were regularly cut by the mint engravers from 1551.[9] Mint engravers were otherwise chiefly occupied making designs for coins. Designing and engraving a Great Seal was a coveted commission for artists of repute, among whom was Isaac Oliver, who devised the Great Seal of Queen Elizabeth I.[10] Engravers of seals were originally paid a salary, but from 1705 the salary was abandoned and fees were paid for the production of individual seals. The fee of £2,500 paid to one engraver for seals of solid silver appears exorbitant until it is understood that he would not be needed again until a new sovereign came to the throne.[11] Thomas Simon (c.1620-1665) was responsible for the execution of a larger number of Great Seals than any other engraver.[12] As chief engraver of the mint he designed seals for Charles I and Oliver Cromwell, and after the Restoration he engraved the Great Seals of Ireland and England for Charles II. Simon's remuneration varied with the change of ruler. Cromwell paid him £43 6s 8d, but Charles II increased his salary to £50, and the artist was otherwise paid for his individual designs.[13] Seal patterns, designed for the three rulers by Simon, are preserved in a book of engravings by George Vertue, published in 1753.[14] Vertue noted that £150 was Simon's fee for the Great Seal which he had engraved for Charles II.[15]

Simon's design for the obverse of Charles II's Great Seal of Ireland is known only from wax impressions of the seal (Plate 2). King Charles, wearing a crown, is shown enthroned under a circular curtained baldachin. The floor appears to be tiled, and the background shows a diaper pattern with alternating roses and harps in cir-

*2 – Impression of the obverse
of the Great Seal of Ireland
of Charles II (pl. xcii in
ARCHAEOLOGIA, lxxxv, 1935)*

cles. The throne is elaborately decorated with a sunburst at the top. The royal arms
appear on a shield at the centre of the sunburst, which is flanked by two heads on
scrolls. The armrests are supported by eagles on carved plinths. The monarch holds
a sceptre in his right hand, and an orb surmounted by a cross in his left hand. His
feet rest on a cushion laid on a circular carpet. A large, crowned rose is to the right
of the King, and on his left there is a crowned harp with angelic fore-pillar. Inside
the carved border, an inscription proclaims the King's dominion over England,
Ireland and France.

Among Vertue's engravings of Simon's works are images of the reverses of
Charles II's Great Seals of Ireland and England (Plates 3, 4). Differences between
the images of the King on the two seals suggest an exercise in propaganda. A tri-
umphant, confident monarch is presented on the English seal (Plate 4). Facing right,
his windswept locks are uncovered and he wears a billowing cloak over his suit of
armour. His expression is benign. The large, brawny, caparisoned horse appears to
be smiling, and its mane and tail are carefully groomed.

On the Great Seal of Ireland, the monarch wears a helmet and is accompanied by a running hound (Plate 3). His rigid posture and vigilant expression suggest
that he is prepared for conflict. The slightly built mount is bare except for the sad-
dle. Its mane is untidy and its facial expression is fearful. On both Great Seals, King
Charles' sword is drawn. It is, however, unaggressively held in a horizontal position

*3 – George Vertue (1684-1756), engraving of the reverse of the Great Seal of Ireland
of Charles II, from a design by Thomas Simon (1620-1665)*

(courtesy National Library of Ireland)

*4 – George Vertue (1684-1756), engraving of the reverse of the Great Seal of England
of Charles II, from a design by Thomas Simon (1620-1665)*

(courtesy National Library of Ireland)

on the English seal; on the Great Seal of Ireland the sword is raised in an alert, defensive gesture. The large mass of Westminster Abbey dominates a densely structured metropolis of large buildings and numerous spires in a scene of London as the background of the English seal. The spire of St Patrick's and the towers of Christ Church can be identified among the sparse array of buildings, arranged around a harbour, in the artist's impression of Dublin on the Irish seal. Some significance may be attached to the numerous ships in Dublin's harbour; there is only one light sailing craft and a few small rowboats in the London scene. Perhaps it is order and tranquillity, contrasted with the bustle and energy which must be expended to impose discipline on the unruly Irish tribes.

There is a crowned harp on the right-hand side of the mounted monarch on the reverse of the Great Seal of Ireland. Richard Hayward states that as a heraldic form representing Ireland, the harp was introduced in the reign of Henry VIII. It replaced 'three crowns in pale' which King Henry deemed inappropriate because it 'looked like a papal tiara'.[16] The harp became an element of the design of the Irish seal in the Elizabethan era, and with Charles I the device assumed the angelic form.[17]

A Great Seal of Ireland, which was in use in the reign of King Edward VII, is in the National Museum of Ireland, Collins Barracks (Plates 5, 6). King Edward's reign extended from 1901 to 1910, during which time two Lords Chancellor, Edward Gibson (Ch. 1895-1905) and Samuel Walker (Ch. 1905-11) held the office in Ireland. Allan Wyon was at that time the engraver of Royal Seals. [18]

A procedure of affixing impressions of the Great Seal to documents took place in chancery with the Chancellor attended by various officers of his department, including a chaffwax and a sealer.[19] Impressions were made by compressing a substance, usually melted wax, between the two parts of the matrix. The chaffwax prepared the wax, and depending on the patent to be confirmed, the wax was coloured green or red.[20] A cord or lace for attachment was laid between the two parts, the composition of which was of some significance (Plate 7):

> In the reign of Anne and perhaps earlier, the seals of Letters patent conferring titles of honour in Ireland were suspended by strings of a more costly character. A duke, a marquis or an Earl, then paid £2. 13. 4d. for gold strings, a viscount paid £2. for gold and silver strings, a baron paid £1. 6s for silver strings and a baronet paid 13s. 4d for strings of silk and silver.[21]

The sealer, using a variety of methods, attached the seal to the document.[22]

The posts of chaffwax and sealer had significant financial benefits. In addi-

---

5, 6 – Obverse and reverse of the Great Seal of Ireland of Edward VII
(courtesy National Museum of Ireland)

7 – Impression of the reverse of the Great Seal of Ireland of Charles II,
with intact attachment cord (courtesy Public Records Office, Kew)

tion to his salary, a chaffwax was paid fees for fuel and oil for tempering the wax. He also had board and travelling allowances. In 1833 it was estimated that an English chaffwax earned £1,272 15s 5d.[23] A sealer's salary for attaching seals was also augmented by sundry levies. He had an allowance for the 'baggs, stamell cloth and towells' used to protect the seal within the Chancellor's purse.[24] He was also paid 'for the carriage, clensing, mending and setting up in court, the instruments used for sealing', and a 'riding charge' of £15 for 'following the Great Seal into the country'.[25] His guaranteed emoluments were such that the sealer eventually ceased to officiate in person, and his duties were passed to a deputy, paid partly by him, whose salary was augmented by gratuities.[26]

In former times, when a new seal was made, the old one was broken into several pieces. It is now the custom to invalidate the seal by defacing it in a ritual called 'damasking', which renders it useless by being tapped with a special hammer, the head of which is indented.[27] The defaced matrix, or one half of it, is usually presented to the Lord Chancellor by the monarch.[28] The Great Seal of Ireland, given into the custody of Chancellor Lord Thomas Wyndham (Ch. 1726-39), was still in his possession at his death, and was mentioned as a bequest in his will.[29] A large piece of plate 'on which the impression of the Great Seal of Ireland under King George the first is engraven' is also mentioned in the will. The plate may be an example of 'seal ware', a term used in the silver business to describe articles made from defaced Great Seals. Each object made from an obsolete seal was usually engraved with the obverse and reverse of the obsolete seal.[30] The Loftus Cup, a standing cup, was made from the Great Seal of Ireland held by Adam Loftus (Ch. 1581-1606), who was in office during the reign of Elizabeth I (Plate 8).[31] A second seal issued to Loftus was, after the death of Elizabeth in 1603, also made into a cup (Plate 9).[32]

The Great Seal held by Sir Richard Cox (Ch. 1703-7) was transformed into a monteith – a bowl, usually silver, in which glasses are hung to cool from a scalloped rim. A monteith is also commonly used as a punch bowl. In a diary he compiled during his term of office, Chancellor Cox gave the following account of his reception of the old seal and its transformation:

> New Seales being sent over the old Great Seale and the Seale of the Common Pleas belonged to me, the former being 100 and the latter 25 ounces of plate, I made both into a handsome Monteth with the Duke of Ormond's arms on one side, and my own on the other, and desire that it, together with the aforesaid box may be preserved in my family as long as may be.[33]

The Cox monteith is currently in the Chicago Museum of Fine Arts. A Latin inscription on the underside of the monteith identifies its origin as a Great Seal of Ireland:

> *Factus ex magnum siligo illustrassimo Iacobo Duce Ormondia locum terreste & Richard Cox milite sumo cancellario Hibernia Anno serenessima Anna Regina Secundo 1703.*

Because wax impressions of seals are brittle and therefore easily broken, documents with intact impressions attached are comparatively rare. In 1935 Jenkinson listed forty existing examples of impressions of the Great Seal of Ireland, stating that there

8 – The Loftus Cup (Elizabeth I)
(courtesy Ulster Museum)

were some good specimens, but regretting the fact that many, alas, were the merest fragments.[34] Efforts were made to counteract this vulnerability by protecting the seal impression in a bag of silk, wool or canvas, or a flat circular box of wood.[35]

Four documents with perfect wax impressions of the Great Seal of Ireland attached have recently been located, one of which, a document of King George III, is reproduced here (Plate 11).[36] These documents are illuminated in the manner of Books of Hours, with miniature paintings in gold and bright colours, and decorative, hand-written script. Overhead, the reigning sovereign's name is inscribed with elaborated capital letters, and a portrait of the king is contained in the initial letter of his forename. The arms of dignitaries holding royal appointments are on either side, and borders are ornamented with floral or leaf designs. On the document of King George III, heraldic devices above the King's title show the royal arms surrounded by banners at the centre. To the right of the arms there is an English rose. Scotland's emblematic symbol, a thistle, is entwined with the rose. Ireland is symbolically represented by a harp in an ornamental frame on the left. On the same document the arms of Chancellor Bowes (Ch. 1757-67) are seen centre-left, and a tribute to him from the King is in the text.[37]

As already stated, the matrix of the Great Seal was traditionally carried in a special purse. If its purpose was unknown the purse might appear to be a superior type of cushion, but the long holding strap identifies its true function. Extant examples of chancellors' purses are rare, but three purses have been located in Ireland (Plates 1, 10).[38] A fourth purse, issued during the tenure of Sir Ignatius O'Brien (Ch. 1913-18), is presently in a private collection in England.

There appears to be no published history relating to the Irish chancellors' purses, but the existing examples and those seen in portraits and on memorials confirm that they are in most aspects of design similar to English chancellors' purses (Plates 12, 13).[39] A common origin is therefore suggested. The earliest record of an English chancellor's purse is a drawing in the margin of a memorandum relating to the seal in an exchequer roll of 1298.[40] The transformation to an elaborately ornamented bag is attributed to Cardinal Wolsey.[41] Wolsey, who was renowned for his love of display, was appointed Lord Chancellor of England by Henry VIII in 1515.

Maxwell-Lyte gives an account of the evolution of the Chancellor's purse.[42] He documents the alteration of the cost of its production from the fourteenth to the eighteenth century, and the frequency of it renewal. He also identifies some of the materials used in the manufacture of the purses, and mentions people who were employed in their embellishment. The

9 – The Loftus Cup (James I)
(courtesy Christie's, London)

59

10 – Lord Chancellor of Ireland's purse from the reign of Queen Victoria
(courtesy Genealogical Office, Dublin)

purse was originally a simple white or red bag of cloth or leather, and was expected to be in use for a considerable time. In 1501, 6s 8d was charged for repairing a purse. The alteration in the size and appearance of the purse resulted in an escalation of the cost of its production. In 1353 the purse cost 6s and in 1415 it was 16s 8d. The price for embroidery, tassels and a strap was £20 5s 8d in 1551. By 1699 the cost had risen to £55, and in 1751 it was £58. Purses delivered in December 1800 and June 1801 each cost £70. The proximity of the two deliveries is likely to be associated with the evolution of Great Britain to the United Kingdom and a con-

11 – Document of George III with seal-impression of the Great Seal of Ireland of George III
(Centre for Kentish Studies, courtesy Lord Brabourne)

sequent alteration in the design of the royal arms. In 1873 the price of the purse
was reduced to £65.

Woollen cloth, velvet and satin were used in the manufacture of the purses. In
1551 the materials consisted of sixteen lengths of green woollen cloth. costing eight
shillings a length. Smaller lengths of crimson velvet and satin were priced at 49s 8d
and 28s 8d. The extant examples and numerous versions in portraits of Lords
Chancellor show that the bodies of the purses were most commonly made of red
cloth. The black velvet used in the manufacture of a purse used by a Lord

Chancellor of Ireland is exceptional (Plate 1).

Men and women were employed to embroider the purses. Jon Parr, appointed in 1581, was Queen Elizabeth I's embroiderer.[43] Continuing his account of the purse, Maxwell-Lyte noted a purse embroidered by Roger Nelham in 1652, and that Francis Greene was responsible for the embroidery on a purse provided in 1751. The two purses already noted as made in the early eighteenth century were delivered by Elizabeth Berry.

In 1652 a purse of crimson velvet was 'ingrained with the arms of the Commonwealth of England at large'.[44] The royal arms continued to be the principal decorative element of the purses, with the reigning monarch identified by his or her initials on either side of the crown which surmounts the arms. An English rose, a thistle for Scotland and some shamrocks for Ireland are part of the design. The arms are framed by a border, the decoration of which includes floral and leaf designs, with winged putti at the corners. On the extant Irish purses, putti, in the centres of the upper and lower borders, are flanked by overflowing cornucopias. Significantly, the symbol at the centre of one or both of the laterals is replaced with a harp on a cushion. The recurrence of this device on purses in portraits of Lords Chancellor of Ireland and on their memorial monuments suggests that it was the distinguishing native symbol (Plates 12, 13).[45]

Embellishment of the purses accorded them some significance in the history of the decorative arts. A purse recently acquired by the British Museum is described as 'one of the most exciting embroideries to be acquired' in recent years.[46] A variety of threads, stitches and appliqué ornaments were used in the process of decoration. In 1652 a purse for the Great Seal of England was embroidered 'with the best double refined gold and silver upon a rich crimson velvet'.[47]

Sequins arranged in circular patterns on a net of chevrons executed in couching, are on the backgrounds of extant Irish purses (Plates 1, 10). Couching is a technique whereby threads or cord are fastened down with stitches made by another thread. Sections of the floral ornaments and the hair of the putti consist of layers of needleweaving, using gold thread. Gold thread is also employed in the formation of the harps. The heads, cornucopias, floral ornaments and the cushions containing the harps are raised to high relief by stump work (padding). Stump work is also used to create the rampant supporters of the royal arms – a crowned lion and a unicorn. The unicorn is bound around its body and one hind leg with an applied length of gold chain. The crown is a mass of crumpled velvet. Pieces of green satin are applied to create shamrocks. Mottoes are stitched in gold thread on an oval of dark material which surrounds the royal crest and on a ribbon made of applied blue satin, woven through the lower section of the arms. The large tassels hanging from the ends of the holding strap are made of gold and coloured threads. The heads of the tassels are

12 – William Dickinson (1746-1823), engraving after Wyndham Madden (fl.1766-75) of James Hewitt, Viscount Lifford, Lord Chancellor of Ireland, 1767-89 (courtesy NGI)

bound with nets made of gold wire.

At sometime in the sixteenth century, a custom evolved whereby a new purse was provided every year.[48] The old purse then became the property of the Chancellor, and curtains, chair covers and fire screens were made from discarded purse, by the wives of chancellors who held office for several years.[49] The custom of a yearly renewal of the purse was discontinued in 1872 after the death of an old lady who had arranged their production, and it was then expected to last for three years.[50]

A business card of Lambert Brown & Clowes (Plate 14), attached to an Irish

13 – John Van Nost (c.1712-80), memorial to John, Lord Bowes, Lord Chancellor of Ireland, 1757-67 (detail)
(courtesy Christ Church Cathedral, Dublin)

opposite
14 – Business card found in a Lord Chancellor of Ireland's purse
(courtesy Genealogical Office, Dublin)

chancellor's purse in the Genealogical Office, Dublin, suggests that the purse may have been made in Ireland.[51] The business is described as 'Gold Lace Manufacturers and Embroidery and Naval Military Outfitters, Cap Makers to the Royal Western Yacht Club of Ireland'. Lambert Brown & Clowes had addresses at 27 Dame Street, Dublin, and 236 Regent Street, London, but the firm no longer operates in either city.

On official occasions the purse was carried before the Chancellor by a purse-bearer, 'an honest and understanding man', who sometimes acted as a secretary.[52] Chancellor Wyndham appointed the poet Ambrose Phillips as his purse-bearer.[53] Michael Foss observed that it was common practice to include great writers and poets among 'place holders', and Phillips is one of the authors mentioned as examples.[54] The accumulative fees for various tasks associated with the post apparently made it a much sought-after situation. John Fitzgibbon's biographer, Anne Kavanaugh, described the position of purse-bearer as 'a lucrative sinecure', which Fitzgibbon (Ch. 1789-1802) bestowed on his nephew John, a member of the 'patronage-glutted Beresfords', at a salary of £700 per annum.[55]

The custom of carrying the purse before the Chancellor persists in England, but it no longer holds the matrix of the Great Seal. The purse is normally empty, but it is used to hold the Queen's speech at the opening of parliament. Although the time when the change took place is unknown, a legendary account attributes it to an accident that occurred in the eighteenth century. The Lord Chancellor of England reputedly dropped the purse containing the seal and it broke a bone in his foot (the weight of the present matrix is eighteen pounds).[56]

The origin of the Chancellor's mace lies in the heavy-headed metal clubs used in battle during the middle ages. The mace eventually evolved into a tall, elegant silver staff, stabilised by the insertion of a wooden shaft and surmounted by a large ornamented head. Decorated with heraldic devices, it gradually became a symbol of power rather than aggression, for persons of importance. For Lords Chancellor it represented regal authority. In his progress to the House of Lords and the Court of Chancery, the mace was carried before the Chancellor by a serjeant-at-arms.[57] It is not known when the office of serjeant-at-arms was established, but a silver mace is noted being borne before Cardinal Wolsey, who was Lord Chancellor of England in the sixteenth century.[58]

The mace presently used in the English House of Lords dates from the time of Charles II; it may therefore be assumed that replacement was not a frequent occurrence.[59] Consequently, the new Chancellor's mace made for the Irish House of Lords in 1766 must be considered an artefact of great importance (Plate 15). An old Irish mace, the origins of which are unknown, was pronounced in the Irish House of Lords in 1766 to be 'quite decayed, and not suitable to the dignity of the House', and Lord Chancellor Bowes was asked to request the sanction of the Lord

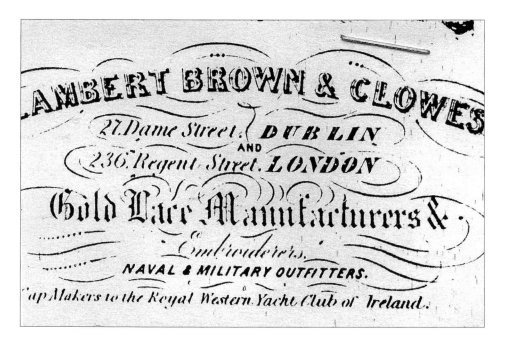

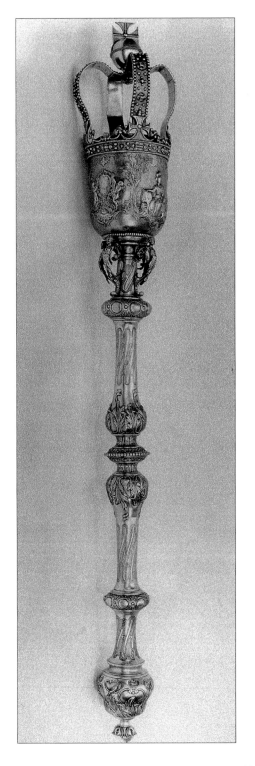

Lieutenant to order a new mace.[60]

The 'new' mace, now in the National Museum of Ireland, is made of silver, and remaining traces indicate that it was originally gilded.[61] It is 148cm long, and is composed of nine separate pieces. The mace is marked in several places with the Harp Crowned and Hibernia – the Dublin hallmark for *c.*1765. The hallmark bears no date letter. It is also marked in several places with the maker's mark W.T. (William Townsend).[62] Townsend's fee for his work is unknown, but on 22 December 1766, Isaac D'Olier, silversmith, who probably secured the commission for Townsend, was paid £286 9s 4.3/4d for the mace.[63]

A wealth of decoration which covers the mace for the whole of its length includes figures, stylised acanthus leaves, scrolls, interlace, fluting and beading. The shaft is interrupted with several bulbous extrusions, and ornaments include plant elements and one circlet of beading. Curved herms, terminating in tapering acanthus leaves and decorated scrolls, spring from the top of the shaft to support the head. On the head, surrounded by symbolic emblems, seated figures of Britannia and Hibernia emphasise the dual authority of England and Ireland. Plumed helmets are worn by both figures, and above each there is a sunburst with a head at the centre. Assisted by

15 – The Lord Chancellor of Ireland's mace (courtesy National Museum of Ireland)

winged cupids, Britannia supports a shield which bears the French arms; her shaft is also held by a cupid. Hibernia holds her staff with her right arm, and with her left hand she supports a shield bearing a harp. Between the human images there is a profusion of plant ornament, and on two shields, supported by putti, the entwined letters GR identify the reigning monarch George III. The royal arms, executed in repoussé, are on the flat top of the head, which is surmounted by a four-ribbon crown with an orb and a cross overhead.[64] The ribbons and the base of the crown are ornamented with a pattern of beading.

The new Irish mace became the property of the Irish Free State when the office of Lord Chancellor of Ireland was abolished. It was deposited in the National Museum of Ireland in 1925 by the Executive Council of Ireland, and is now permanently exhibited in the National Museum at Collins Barracks, Dublin.[65]

To emphasise his personal stature and the dignity of his occupation, the Lord Chancellor eventually assumed a distinctive mode of dress. Churchmen, who were the original holders of the office of Lord Chancellor, would have worn their 'ecclesiastical robes or their episcopal Parliamentary robes'.[66] In the preface to his *Lives of the Lords Chancellors of Ireland*, Roderick O'Flanagan noted that the earliest Chancellor's robe was 'a green tunic of a woman, with a cape of the same colour'. O'Flanagan attributes the description to Matthew Paris, but does not name the source of the information.[67]

The black gown trimmed with gold lace which became the familiar attire of Lords Chancellor is, with minor differences, the ceremonial attire for a number of dignitaries: these include the Speaker of the House of Commons, the Chancellor of the Exchequer, and heads of universities. The robe is usually made of the finest black damask – a figured silk or linen material – believed to have originated from the city of Damascus. Three-inch-wide bands of gold lace and other gold ornaments are affixed to the robe by hand. The gown originated in the sixteenth century, at which time it may have been 'a rich form of lay fashion for those of outstanding dignity'.[68]

Christopher Allen states that the exclusivity of chancellors' robes was probably a consequence of the Sumptuary Laws introduced in the Tudor period. One of the laws stipulated that certain types of material and embellishments could be worn only by people of elevated social standing. Subsequently, senior officers of state assumed ornate versions of standard robes as signifiers of their authority.[69]

Allen also documented the following evolution of the ornaments that adorn chancellors' robes.[70] In the seventeenth century, Francis Bacon, Lord Chancellor of England, wore a gown trimmed with gold braid. A century later robes were embellished with hand-made lace manufactured from gold wire. The lace, affixed by hand, was used on the facings of the robe and continued around the lower end. Two rows

Given By Lord Redesdale 1803.

16 – Sir Thomas Lawrence (1769-1830), John Mitford, Lord Redesdale,
Lord Chancellor of Ireland (Ch. 1802-06) (courtesy Westminster Palace, London)

of lace were affixed to the openings of the sleeves, and there were four rows above the opening. Lace decorations were also attached to the wings of the shoulders. Gold buttons, formerly used to fasten the sleeves, eventually evolved into ornamental toggles. Allen observed that no tradition of design emerged in the manufacture of the lace, and inspection of portraits of Irish and English chancellors shows great variety in the creation of patterns (Plates 12, 16). The uniformity in the number of rows of gold lace attached to the gowns, indicated by Allen, is not evident in portraits of Lords Chancellor of Ireland. The non-conformity may, however, be indicative of artistic creation.

The richness of the cloth and the value of the gold ornaments must have made the purchase of a gown a costly investment for a chancellor. Allowances of £1,000 granted by the monarch to Richard West in 1725 and to Thomas, Lord Wyndham in 1726 'towards the Equipage and Preparation for the Employment of Chancellor', may be relevant to the cost of such attire.[71] A similar grant made to John, Baron Fitzgibbon in 1789 suggests that inflation was not a problem in the eighteenth century.[72]

The business card of Lambert Brown & Clowes, found in the Chancellor's purse in the Irish Genealogical Office, states that one of their occupations was the manufacturing of gold lace. It should, therefore, be considered possible that the firm was responsible for the production and affixing of the gold lace to chancellors' robes.

There is evidence that when he died, a chancellor's robe was considered an article of such value that it became a desired inheritance. Thomas Lord Wyndham bequeathed his 'Chancellor's velvet gown trimmed with gold' to Mr Matthew 'for having always had the care of it in Ireland'.[73] In her will, the widowed Viscountess Lifford assigned her late husband's robe of office to her son, who had inherited the title of Viscount Lifford.[74]

The accoutrements of the Lords Chancellor of Ireland appear for the most part to have faded into obscurity with the annulment of the office. However, portraits of the chancellors continue to remind us of the grandeur and pomp annexed to the title. Although the Lord Steward's white rod was destroyed at the close of trials of peers, it is an accessory in a portrait of Thomas, Lord Wyndham (Ch. 1626-39).[75] In the majority of the portraits the sitters are attired in the gold-trimmed gown and mandatory long wig, with the purse and mace occupying a salient position in the composition. Two instances of a desire for preservation of a chancellor's gown have been noted, but there is no evidence of concurrence with those hopes. The existing Irish purses, though possibly made in England, are fine examples of complicated traditional needlework. Variations in the illustration of the mace in portraits suggest artistic invention, but the sculpted mace on the memorial of

Chancellor Bowes, who requested the new mace, is an acceptable reproduction of the original. The extant mace demonstrates the skills of an eighteenth-century Irish silversmith.

The Chancellor's most important definition of authority was the Great Seal of Ireland, and the only known extant example is Edward VII's Great Seal, now in the National Museum. King Edward was the penultimate English monarch to govern Ireland. Since outdated seals were sometimes melted down and made into alternative objects, the extant seal must be one of the Irish museum's most prestigious acquisitions. It is a fine example of silver engraving. Otherwise, the designs of Great Seals of Ireland can be deduced from Vertue's engraving of Thomas Simon's designs for the seal of Charles II, and existing seal impressions.

———

ACKNOWLEDGEMENTS

I would like to acknowledge assistance given by Colum McCabe, Helen McCabe, Prof Michael McCarthy, Vera Murtagh, Dr Brendan O'Donoghue, Dr Michael Kenny, Dr Conor O'Brien and Alison Fitzgerald.

ENDNOTES

[1] Brehon is a derivative of the Irish *breitheamh*, meaning judge.
[2] National Museum, register no. 21, 1925, 113. The office was abolished by the Courts of Justice Act 1924, Section 19.
[3] Roderick O'Flanagan, *Lives of the Lord Chancellors and Keepers of the Great Seal of Ireland, from the Earliest Times to the Reign of Queen Victoria*, 2 vols (London 1870). The ceremonials associated with trials of peers is described in ii, 69-70.
[4] Maurice Bond and David Beamish, *The Lord Chancellor* (London 1977) 18.
[5] Hilary Jenkinson, 'The Great Seal of England: Deputed or Department Seals', *Archaeologia*, lxxxv (1935) 314.
[6] *ibid.* Jenkinson's theories were based on information gleaned from an untitled article by F.W. Maitland, *Collected Papers* (Cambridge 1911).
[7] Bond and Beamish, *The Lord Chancellor*, 22.
[8] *The Times*, 15 January 1801 (London): 'Friday the Great Seal of Ireland being delivered up to his Excellency the Lord Lieutenant by the Right Hon. Arthur Lord Viscount Kilwarden, C.J.K.B. and Baron Viscount Avonmore C.B.I., two of the Lords Commissioners for keeping the Great Seal of Ireland, in the Lord Chancellor's absence, the same was defaced in his Excellency's presence, and his Excellency was thereupon pleased to deliver to their Lordships a new Great Seal of the United Kingdom to be used in that part of the United Kingdom called Ireland, and to direct that the same be made use of (*pro tempore*) for sealing all things whatev-

er which pass the Great Seal'.

[9] John Craig, *The Mint* (Cambridge 1953) 201.

[10] A list of engravers of Great Seals is given in vol. 2 of William J. Hocking, *Catalogue of the Coins, Tokens, Medals, Dies and Seals in the Museum of the Royal Mint* (London 1910) 279.

[11] John Craig, *The Mint*, 201.

[12] Hocking, *Catalogue*, 297.

[13] John Pinkerton, *And Essay on Medals*, 2 vols (London 1808) ii, 171.

[14] George Vertue, *Medals, Coins, Great Seals and other Works of Thomas Simon* (London 1753, 2nd edition).

[15] Vertue, *Works of Thomas Simon*, 92.

[16] Richard Hayward, *The Story of the Irish Harp* (Dublin 1954) 13.

[17] *ibid.* The term 'angelic' refers to the human winged figure which forms the fore-pillar.

[18] Hocking, *Catalogue*, 297.

[19] H.C. Maxwell-Lyte, *Historical Notes on the use of the Great Seal of England* (London 1926) 264-98.

[20] Bond and Beamish, *The Lord Chancellor*, 23.

[21] Maxwell-Lyte, *Historical Notes*, 301.

[22] *ibid.*, 300-05.

[23] *ibid.*, 292.

[24] *ibid.*, 290. 'Four bags of "buckes leather" and four bags of coarse, red cloth called "stamell" were it appears, considered necessary for the protection of the Great Seal within its embroidered purse'. The 'towells' were used for cleaning the Great Seal from oil and wax.

[25] *ibid.*

[26] *ibid.*

[27] Bond and Beamish, *The Lord Chancellor*, 21.

[28] *ibid.*

[29] Wiltshire Records Office, document no. 234/16. Copy of the will of Thomas Lord Wyndham, dated 29 July 'To my nephew, Sir Wyndham Knatchbull the late King's Great Silver Seal of Ireland as broken in the Privy Council of Ireland, and a desire that it may be left in his family as a remembrance of me'.

[30] Harold Newman, *An Illustrated Dictionary of Silverware* (London 1987) 297. Thomas, Lord Wyndham (Ch. 1726-39) held seals for George I and George II.

[31] *ibid.*, 198.

[32] *ibid.* (mark: WI, Christie's, London, 2 December 1981).

[33] Richard Caulfield (ed.), *Autobiography of the Right Honourable Sir Richard Cox Bart, Lord Chancellor of Ireland* (London and Cork 1860) 19. In 1860 the Cox monteith was in the house of the Hon Villiers Stuart of Castletown, county Kilkenny, the property of his wife who had inherited it from her brother, the late Sir Richard Cox. The box mentioned was given to Cox when, on Saturday, 4 December 1703, 'the Lord Mayor, Recorder, Alderman and Sheriff of Dublin, came to my house and presented me with my freedom to the citty in a gold box, which cost 30*Li.*, and wished me many years enjoyment of my office'.

[34] Jenkinson, *The Great Seal*, 316.

[35] Maxwell-Lyte, *Historical Notes*, 312.

[36] Patricia McCabe, *Images of Law and Order, Accoutrements, Carriage, Portraits and Memorials of Lords Chancellor of Ireland, 1660-1860*, 3 vols, unpublished PhD thesis, 2002,

iii, pls 200-03.

[37] Centre for Kentish Studies, Maidstone, document no. F5, 'our [the King's] Right Trusty and Well beloved Counsellor John Baron Bowes of Clonlyon; our Chancellor of our said Kingdom of Ireland'. This was the only document among the four mentioned which was available for close inspection. It concerns the elevation of Kenneth Mackenzie to Baron and Viscount.

[38] The third example, a purse of Queen Victoria's reign, is in Malahide Castle, county Dublin.

[39] See also the Jocelyn memorial in Great St Mary's Church, Sawbridgeworth, and the Wyndham monument in Salisbury Cathedral in McCabe, *Images of Law and Order*, iii, pls 111, 190.

[40] Maxwell-Lyte, *The Great Seal*, 318.

[41] Bond and Beamish, *The Lord Chancellor*, 34.

[42] Maxwell-Lyte, *The Great Seal*, 318-19.

[43] Anne Wanner, 'Textiles in History', *British Museum Newsletter*, 5 (London 1997).

[44] Maxwell-Lyte, *The Great Seal*, 319.

[45] The purses in portraits are not all as described above. The alternative designs may be artistic invention, or perhaps if portraits were executed in England, the pattern of an English chancellor's purse may have been used.

[46] Wanner, *BM Newsletter*.

[47] Maxwell-Lyte, *The Great Seal*, 319.

[48] *ibid.*, 318.

[49] Bond and Beamish, *The Lord Chancellor*, 36.

[50] *ibid.*

[51] The information was made available from the archives of the Genealogical Office, Kildare Street, Dublin, by John Farrell, with the permission of Brendan O'Donoghue, Chief Herald.

[52] Maxwell-Lyte, *The Great Seal*, 264.

[53] *Dublin Weekly Journal*, 24 December 1726.

[54] Michael Foss, *The Age of Patronage, Arts in Society 1660-1750* (London 1971) 141.

[55] Anne Kavanaugh, *John Fitzgibbon, Earl of Clare* (Dublin 1997) 209.

[56] Bond and Beamish, *The Lord Chancellor*, 36.

[57] *ibid.*

[58] *ibid.*, 32.

[59] *ibid.*, 34.

[60] *Journals of the Irish House of Lords*, iv, 2 May 1766, 377.

[61] Information from Dr Michael Kenny, director of the NMI.

[62] Information from Conor O'Brien who is preparing a catalogue for a forthcoming exhibition in the NMI silver galleries.

[63] 'An Account of Money expended under the Head of Concordium from Lady-day 1765 to Lady-day 1767', *Journals of the Irish House of Commons*, lviii (1771) appendix 2, cxxx.

[64] NMI, register no. 21, 1925, file mo. 30 A 1, 1925. In the entry for the mace it is stated that the 'fleur de lys cresting and orb and cross are missing'. The orb and cross presently on the mace are believed to be restoration additions. Information from Michael Kenny, Assistant Keeper NMI, Collins Barracks.

[65] *ibid.*

[66] Bond and Beamish, *The Lord Chancellor*, 36.

[67] O'Flanagan, *Lives of the Lord Chancellors*, 15.

[68] W.N. Hargreaves-Mawdsley, *History of Legal Dress in Europe* (Oxford 1963) 68.

[69] Christopher Allan, 'Theatre of State', unpaginated, unpublished essay (London 1999). C. Allan is Specialist Operations Co-ordinator at Ede & Ravenscroft Robemakers, London, a firm established in 1689 during the reign of William and Mary.

[70] *ibid.*

[71] *Journals of the Irish House of Commons*, v (1723-30); West, 510, Wyndham, 513.

[72] *ibid.*, lxvi, 1 Feb 1790, appendix 3, ccxci. The £1,000 0s 0d granted to John Fitzgibbon, described as 'his Majesty's free Gift', towards his Equipage and preparation for the Employment of Chancellor' was remitted on 30 July 1789.

[73] Wiltshire Records Office, document no. 234/16 in Knatchbull Papers, Will of Thomas Wyndham, 29 July 1745, codicil, 2 September 1745.

[74] Coventry Records Office, Hewitt Family Papers, document no. 1484/8/1.

[75] McCabe, *Images of Law and Order*, iii, pl. 185.

———

From Venice to Monasterevin: the altar rails in the Church of Sts Peter and Paul

BEATRICE WHELAN

T HE CHURCH OF STS PETER AND PAUL IN MONASTEREVIN, COUNTY KILDARE, invites curiosity for many reasons. Built during the Famine, when work at many other parish churches in the country was interrupted, and containing some noteworthy nineteenth-century ceiling paintings, the church has much to offer the art or architectural historian. But perhaps the most interesting feature of the church is the set of eighteenth-century Italian altar rails, which survived Vatican II renovations and have a complex and detailed history of their own.

Though practically no parish records pertaining to the Church of Sts Peter and Paul survive, the history of the church can be pieced together from newspaper and other accounts of building progress. The laying of the foundation stone on 26 August 1840, and the first Mass held in the church on 29 August 1847 are noted in the baptism records of the parish.[1] On 31 October 1840 a chancery advertisement relating to the land that the church was built on is recorded in the *Leinster Express*. In 1849 the architect of the church, William Deane Butler (1794-1858), exhibited a drawing entitled A *new R.C. Church now being erected at Monasterevin* at the Royal Hibernian Academy of Arts.[2] In 1855-6, on his tour of Ireland, Thomas Lacy of Wexford visited Monasterevin and devoted an entire page to the Church of Sts Peter and Paul in his account of his travels.[3] Lacy found the church to be 'one of the finest buildings to be seen in any town of this class in Ireland'. Lacy's description of the church is a detailed and reliable one, which becomes very important in the absence of other primary documents relating to the church. Lacy's account gives the only reference to the lofty altar screen once inside the church, which not one of the surviving photographs of the interior shows. This altar screen may have remained in the church until the arrival of the marble altar rails in 1880, which all the old photographs of the interior reveal. The year 1879-80 saw the church undergo a period of decoration, which included the painting of the interior walls and sanctuary vault,

1 – The last cherub on the right altar rail in the Church of Sts Peter and Paul, Monasterevin

the addition of new marble main and side altars, and the commissioning of new stained glass windows for the entire church. It was at this time that the church received the set of altar rails which investigation reveals came from the Church of S. Stefano in Venice.

The altar rails in the church consist of two railings on either side of the steps leading to the main altar (Plates 2, 3). They are both 455cm (14ft 11in) in length and 86cm (2ft 10in) in height. Four types of stone are used in their construction. The base and top consist of Giallo di Siena marble; between these are balusters of Rosso Antico. There are twenty-four full balusters in all, twelve on each rail, and eight half balusters, four on each rail. Separating the complete balusters into groups of six are cherubs carved in Carrara marble in various poses, and holding corn, grapes and a type of flower, which has the appearance of a rose (Plates 1, 6, 7). The cherubs, which are in high relief, are set against rectangular blocks of stone composed of the same beige stone as the base and top. A black marble veneer, contrasting with the white Carrara of the cherubs, serves as a background to them.

The altar rails carry a Latin inscription, and close examination suggests that it survives in its complete and original form. The inscription reads: *MAGISTER . FR . AVGVSTINVS . CORNEAVS . V . EXPROV . POS . A . 1712 .*

Prof Damien Nelis and Prof Andrew Smith of the Classics departments in

2 – The left altar rail in the Church of Sts Peter and Paul

Trinity College and University College Dublin examined the inscription and came to similar conclusions. Prof Smith advised me that the inscription probably read as follows: 'Magister Fr[ater] Augustinus Corneaus V[icarius] Exprov[incialis] pos[uit] a[nno] 1712' (i.e. 'Master Brother Augustinus Corneaus Vicar Exprovincial set up [these altar rails] in the year 1712').

Stylistically we may assume that the date of manufacture is close to 1712. Prof Smith also suggests that 'magister' may indicate the academic rank of the person who set up the altar rails, and that 'frater' (brother) is a term used for friars even if they are ordained priests, and therefore that this man may well have been an Augustinian friar. It is most likely that the inscription gives the name and titles of the friar who set up the altar rails in 1712.

Apart from the inscription there are no other markings on the rails. For further information other contemporary sources are vital, such as the publication *Some Notable Conversions in the county of Wexford by the Revd Francis J. Kirk*.[4] This book provides an account of how notable people in Wexford converted to the Catholic faith in the mid and later nineteenth century. Much of the book concerns the conversion of a leading family of Gorey, the Ram family, with whom Kirk was well acquainted. It is in the course of his description of the family's estate of Ramsfort in Gorey that Kirk mentions the altar rails. He wrote:

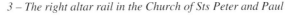

3 – The right altar rail in the Church of Sts Peter and Paul

The old family mansion had been burned during the rebellion of 1798, and in consequence of the disturbed state of the country no effort was made by the family to rebuild it. Stephen's father was the first of his family to attempt rebuilding but died before the house was finished. His son was well qualified to carry on the work: his tastes were refined and artistic. Large sums of money were required to carry out his plans; objects of ancient and modern art were collected from all parts of the Continent; rare manuscripts and antique jewellery formed a unique private collection.

Notable among these treasures was an altar rail of Siena and other precious marbles bought by him in Italy, which for more than a century had been the ornament of an Italian church. This beautiful work of art was placed by him on a terrace leading to the pleasure grounds. After remaining there for several years it was purchased by a Protestant gentleman, who intended to place it in a church built in his own grounds; but happily, finding it much too large for the position, he sold it at a moderate price to the parish priest of Monasterevin, Co Kildare, so that it now fulfils the purpose for which it was originally intended.[5]

Kirk's account is supported by two photographs of the 'pleasure grounds' of Ramsfort (Plates 4, 5).[6] One photograph (Plate 4) shows the altar rails (from a distance) in front of the house, just above the flight of steps. The other shows the gardens, with a cherub of the rails seen on either side of the photograph (Plate 5). The positions of at least two of the cherubs on the altar rails have changed since they were at Ramsfort. This can be seen by comparing the cherubs shown on the Ramsfort photograph (Plate 5) with the cherubs in Monasterevin (Plate 6). The difference is clear, as each of the cherubs is distinctive. By comparing photographs we can see that the first cherub on the right rail was not moved and still holds that position. The last cherub on the left rail (Plate 6), however, did not have that position at Ramsfort. There the last cherub on the left rail was the cherub which is now the last cherub on the right rail (Plates 1, 5). This changing of positions possibly occurred when the rails were being installed in the church at Monasterevin, and may have been done deliberately, resulting in a more symmetrical arrangement. The cherubs now look and turn inwards and face each other across the opening in the rails (Plate 6). The many cracks in the rails and the visible mortar imply that the rails were simply taken apart upon their removal from Ramsfort and then reassembled when they reached their destination.

From newspaper reports we know that the rails had been bought for the church in Monasterevin by 1879, but the question remains as to how long they had been absent from Ramsfort at this date, and where they had been in the intervening

4 – View of Ramsfort House and gardens, Gorey, county Wexford (c.1871-72)

5 – View of Ramsfort gardens: the cherubs on the altar rails can be seen to the left and right
(courtesy Michael Fitzpatrick)

6 – The altar rails in the Church of Sts Peter and Paul

7 – The first cherub on the left altar rail in the Church of Sts Peter and Paul

period. The two photographs which show the rails at Ramsfort (Plates 4, 5) seem to be a pair of the same date, but this date is disputed. Dan Walsh has dated them to 1886.[7] The three stages of building at Ramsfort House are very evident from changes in its style of architecture (Plate 4). It is the third wing, with its ground-floor arcade and circular turret, that is important to the dating of the photograph. Walsh's date for the third wing of 1871-72 would suit the appearance of the rails in the photograph. If the rails were still at Ramsfort in 1872, then they were still there when Stephen Ram sold the property in 1870.[8] Ramsfort was bought by William Kirk, brother of Francis J. Kirk.[9] It was probably William Kirk who sold the rails to the 'Protestant gentleman' who, according to Francis Kirk, sold them to the parish priest of Monasterevin. William Kirk no doubt told his brother what happened to the rails; thus we can trust the authenticity of Francis Kirk's account.

It is not clear for how long the rails were in the possession of the 'Protestant gentleman'. A local Monasterevin historian, Eileen Ryan, wrote an account of the church, informing us of the altar rails that 'this artistic masterpiece was brought to Wexford by the Ram family. Some years later it was purchased from the Adaire family of Rathdare by the Rev Michael Comerford, parish priest of Monasterevin (1878-1895)'.[10] The vendors were John George Adaire (1823-1885) and his wife Cornelia,who called their estate in county Laois, Rathdare. John George Adaire was a Protestant landlord who owned land in counties Donegal, Tipperary, Kilkenny, Kildare and Laois.[11] Was he the same 'Protestant gentleman' of Kirk's account? There is indeed a church at Rathdare, though the rails would not have suited it styl-istically, and it was built by Cornelia in 1887 after John George Adaire had died. Perhaps John George Adaire had hoped to build this in his own lifetime and had bought the rails for that reason, but not having succeeded, sold the rails to the parish of Monasterevin which was then decorating the interior of the church. The only con-nection between the Adaire family and Monasterevin is that John George Adaire's father is listed among the nobility of Monasterevin in *Pigot's Directory* of 1824. Rathdare is relatively close to Monasterevin, and John George Adaire could easily have heard that the church at Monasterevin was undergoing decoration and needed new altar rails. The contemporary newspaper reports that record the placement of the rails in the church do not mention from whom they were bought.

The first mention of the altar rails in connection with Monasterevin is the report on the church in the *Leinster Express* on 25 October 1879, which says that 'a splendid set of Sienna marble communion rails will complete this portion of the sacred edifice'. So, by October 1879, the rails had been acquired but had not yet been placed in the church. A report on the church in the *Leinster Express* of 4 September 1880, repeated in the *Irish Builder* on 15 September, comments on the newly installed rails, saying:

> The principal features in the new church are the communion railings, which have a history all their own. Hundreds of years ago they occupied a similar position in one of the Roman churches, and have since undergone numberless changes. The upper and lower pieces are Giallo di Siena, while the balusters are Rosso antico. Ensconced in these are angels of Carrara marble, some bearing wheat and others flowers. This ancient marble has a most venerable appearance, and bears the imprint of its rare value on its face.

A similar report in the *Leinster Leader* on the same day is more accurate than the *Express*, and rightly acknowledges that they came from the church of S. Stefano in Venice.[12] This brings us to the question of the ultimate origin of the altar rails, and the question of when they were taken from there to be bought by Stephen Ram. Ram travelled extensively and was an avid art collector. One gains a true sense of this from the Rev Kirk's book in which he writes about a journey that he made around Europe in 1854 with Stephen Ram and his wife. Kirk repeatedly recalls how Stephen Ram knew well all the places they visited, especially when it came to buying art treasures. When they visited Genoa, for example, Kirk recalls how

> the time was chiefly spent by Mr. Ram in hunting out curios. He seemed to know every corner of the town. Passing down a narrow slummy street, he knew where to find some old fellow, probably a Jew, who he was sure had something worth looking at ... the visit ended by his purchasing a small illuminated manuscript Office Book, for which he gave £10 ... his refined taste for every kind of art was a misfortune to himself, as he could not refrain from buying what he admired.[13]

Could it have been in some similar circumstance that Stephen Ram purchased the altar rails for his new house at Gorey? Stephen Ram returned from France in 1846 to continue his father's rebuilding of Ramsfort. We can therefore assume that the altar rails were bought by Stephen Ram around or close to1846, or perhaps on the trip he made around Europe in 1854.

The same Thomas Lacy who visited Monasterevin in 1856, later providing an invaluable account of the church, also visited Ramsfort on his travels. It is not clear when exactly he visited Wexford, though it was soon after the rebuilding there. Lacy was a native of Wexford, and Stephen Ram was a subscriber to his book. As we saw in his account of the church, Lacy was more than a casual visitor, and it is possible that he could have spoken with Ram when he visited Ramsfort. Lacy gives a detailed description in which he too notices the altar rails that were to catch Kirk's eye:

> Fine terraces, sloping downwards to the beautiful expanse of water formed by the river Bann, extend for the distance of a furlong on both sides of the

valley, which stretches north and south before the front of the mansion, with various flights of stairs leading to the splendid gardens and elegant parterres that are formed on each side of the intersecting stream.

These terraces, flights of stairs and stream can be seen on the 1872 photograph of Ramsfort's gardens (Plate 4). Lacy then goes on to mention the altar rails:

> The balustrades of the flight immediately in front of the centre of the man-sion [in Monsaterevin] are of finely veined marble, and up to a comparatively recent period, formed some of the ornamental portions of the church of St. Stephano at Venice, where, upon their removal from their original destina-tion, they were purchased by Mr. Ram. Above the summit of the range on each side of the entrance to this flight, stands an elegant allegorical bronze statue, of the most exquisite symmetry.

Lacy's description of the grounds with the railings matches the image on the 1872 photographs, even down to the bronzes on either side of the altar rails (Plate 4). Lacy's claim that the rails came from S. Stefano is confirmed by the report in the *Leinster Leader* on 4 September 1880, and is further confirmed when we delve into the history of S. Stefano.

The church of S. Stefano, built by the Hermits of St Augustine in the thir-teenth century, was rebuilt in the fourteenth century, and in the fifteenth century received 'new additions and alterations and new sculptural and decorative ornamen-tation'.[14] The Gothic interior which resulted consists of nave and side aisles divided by columns of alternating red and white marble. The church has no transepts, and a polygonal apse encloses the church at the east end.[15] Lorenzetti informs us that in the nave, towards the chancel, there was originally a choir, which was demolished in 1613. Its wooden stalls were placed behind the high altar and the marble screen divided and placed around the walls of the chancel. Then the building of a great new altar began, its parapet and the plinths of its columns being decorated with 'inlaid coloured marble' and dating to 1656.[16]

Initially this seems too early for the erection of the altar rails, which, due to their inscription, are firmly dated to 1712. However, a monograph on the Church of S. Stefano written by a Ferdinando Apollonio in 1911, reveals that the erection of the altar rails in 1712 was the completion of the work on the new altar which had begun in 1613: 'The idea of the construction of the new presbytery was born around 1610 ... the choir and the old altar were demolished ... and the altar was brought to the majestic grandeur which we see to-day'.[17] Apollonio goes on to describe in detail the construction of the altar area, and finally concludes,

> Enclosing the presbytery is a balustrade of fine marble. Two gates of worked

iron open in the middle and around the balustrade is the name of Fr. Agostino Corniani who commissioned it: Mag.Fr. Angustinus Cornianus. V. ex Prov. Ann. MDCCXII.[18]

Apollonio transcribes the inscription somewhat inaccurately, and spells the friar's name 'Cornianus' instead of 'Corneaus', as it actually appears on the rails in Monasterevin. Writing in 1911 Apollonio could no longer see the altar rails. For his information Apollonio was relying on a manuscript account of the church written by Agostino Nicolai between about 1752 and 1762, entitled *Memoria Manoscritta Sopra la Chiesa e Monistero di S. Stefano in Venezia*, now in the Correr Library in Venice.[19] Apollonio's version of the inscription on the rails replicates that given by Nicolai. The manuscript account, too, starts by discussing the beginning of the erection of the new altar in 1610, and in relation to the altar rails says:

> The last religious of this monastery who with money of their own use added decoration to the altar were M(agister) F(ra) Giovanni Ferra and M(agister) F(ra) Agostino Corniani, both Venetian and sons of the convent ... the second (of the two) M(agister) Corniani, had the presbytery enclosed with the most beautiful balustrade of fine marble and gates of worked iron, on the top cornice of the said balustrade, one can see written: Mag. Augustinus Cornianus V. ex Prov. An. MDCCX.

This confirms that the rails were commissioned and paid for by an Agostino Corniani, who was an Augustinian friar at the convent of S. Stefano. It does seem that the friar's first name was Agostino, and so when the inscription on the rails uses the word 'Augustinus', it means it in this sense and not as an adjective to mean that he is an Augustinian friar, though Agostino may well have taken this name on entering the order. As for his second name, the written sources spell it 'Corniani', while the inscription on the actual rail spells it 'Corneaus'. I would propose that this may simply be the Latinised spelling of his name. Jennifer Montagu has advised me that the name Corniani would be much more plausible than Corneaus.[20] The Corniani were a successful Venetian family. The entry on Giovanni Giacomo Corniani (1631-1707) in the *Dizionario Biografico degli Italiani* shows the Corniani to have been a prominent legal family whose original name was Rocco. In 1649 the family received recognition of citizenship, which was necessary for entry into the Council of Two Hundred. Giovanni himself had a career in the Venetian senate, while his brother Bernardino undertook an ecclesiastical career, becoming Bishop of Pola.[21] Could Agostino Corniani have been a brother or nephew of these men?

The commissioning of the altar rails around 1712 was one of many new projects carried out for the church of S. Stefano in the early eighteenth century.[22] The

Altar of Sta Monica, the second altar in the right aisle, which was renewed in 1734, provides us with a direct comparison for the altar rails and a possibility of artistic attribution (Plates 8, 9). On the front of the altar table are two putti, carved in high relief from Carrara marble and set against slabs of a greyish-black marble, surrounded by a brownish-beige stone frame, materials noticeably similar to those of the altar rails (Plates 1, 7). Dr Victoria Avery has commented:

> stylistically and formally, these two putti appear similar to those on the altar rails – their physiognomies, their rather 'rubber-like limbs', their poses and the way they clasp their attributes and stand on a small bed of puffy clouds [make it] quite possible that they may be by the same sculptor.[23]

To Dr Avery's comparisons I would add that the facial types of the two putti on the Sta Monica altar table are very similar to the facial types of the altar rail putti, and I would conclude that the artist who sculpted the altar rails in 1712, twenty years later, sculpted the Altar of Sta Monica for the same church.

Merkel has tentatively assigned the putti on the Altar of Sta Monica to the circle of Giovanni Comin (c.1645-1708).[24] Comin was an artist from Treviso, who spent his career as a sculptor there and in Venice. His first documented work is the Altar of the Innocenti (1679) in Sta Giustina, Padua, which exhibits the Baroque influence of sculptors like Jossé de Corte (1627-79), whose works were to be seen in Venice, and Enrigo Meregno (1628-1723), a follower of de Corte. Comin actually worked with Meregno in Venice to execute the statue of *St Luke and a Bishop Saint* for the church of S Nicolo.[25] Comin is closely associated with Meregno, and Dr Montagu has pointed out a similarity between the putti in Meregno's Pietà group in the chapel of the Monte di Pietà in Udine, and the putti of the altar rails.[26] Though the putti of Comin's Altar of the Innocenti and those of Meregno's Pietà group are somewhat similar to the putti on the altar rails, the resemblance is not strong enough to propose that a pupil of either Comin or Meregno was responsible for the altar rails.

Another possible candidate for the putti of the altar rail is the sculptor Orazio Marinali (1634-1720), who trained in Venice with de Corte and carried out numerous religious works throughout the Veneto,[27] but as his monument to Alexander VIII in the Duomovecchio in Breschia shows, his putti, while similar to those on the altar rails, do not bear a significant stylistic resemblance to them. What Comin, Meregno and Marinalli all have in common is that they each trained under, or were influenced by de Corte, and, in fact, de Corte's putti bear the strongest stylistic resemblance to those on the altar rails and on the Altar of Sta Monica. This can especially be seen in his most celebrated work – the high altar in the church of Sta Maria della Salute in Venice (1670).[28] On the base of the altar are putti sculpted in high relief, which have much in common with the putti of the altar rails and the Altar of Sta Monica

8 – The Altar of Sta Monica, the second altar in the right nave of S. Stefano, Venice
(photo V Avery)

(bottom left) 9 – Cherub on the Altar of Sta Monica (photo V Avery)

(bottom right) 10 – Jossé de Corte, putti on the base of the high altar of Sta Maria della Salute,
Venice (courtesy Conway Library, Courtauld Institute)

(Plate 8), though there are considerable differences. It could even be suggested that the Altar of Sta Monica is somewhat modelled on the lower section of de Corte's high altar in Sta Maria della Salute. I would therefore conclude that it was a young pupil of de Corte who sculpted the putti of the altar rails and those of the Altar of Sta Monica, or at least a sculptor who was looking to Jossé de Corte. This pupil did not rigidly conform to de Corte's formula for putti: whereas de Corte's putti stand on rigid oval bases, the putti of the S. Stefano master, as we shall call him, gracefully pose on puffy clouds and so do not need wings, as De Corte's putti do (Plate 10). It is possible that this artist was also influenced by the work of Giovanni Comin, as Merkel has suggested. Certainly Comin's arrangement of his putti on sculpted clouds would suggest a possible influence, but that is the only similarity between the two which I can see. Without a signature on the altar rails or on the Altar of Sta Monica, and with no mention of the artist in the written sources which mention the two pieces, no further artistic attribution can be made. We seem to be dealing with a sculptor who perhaps specialised in carving putti, and so maybe was not considered important enough for a mention in the sources, and who perhaps did not think himself significant enough to sign his pieces.

The altar rails remained in their position in S. Stefano until the mid-nineteenth century when the baroque decoration of the church was no longer in taste. Apollonio, writing in 1911, describes how

> from 1847-1852, the parish priest M.r can. Luigi Piccini, began to restore the church. For this restoration a lot of money was needed which he got from generous parishioners ... he took away the balustrade of the choir and sold them, substituting them for a railing of wood.[29]

The rails were probably sold onto a dealer, from whom Stephen Ram bought them for his new house at Gorey. It seems a lucky paradox that the altar rails ended up in a Gothic revival church which was finished in 1847, the same year in which the priest of S. Stefano began his restorations of the church and removed the rails, as he felt they did not suit the original Gothic interior of the church.

———

ACKNOWLEDGEMENTS

I would like to thank Dr Edward McParland for his continuous support and encouragement throughout the entire research process. Special thanks are due to Basil Phelan for information on Ramsfort House, Michael Fitzpatrick for photographs of Ramsfort gardens, Dr Victoria Avery for her interest and her efforts in Venice, Dr Catherine Lawless for translating many Italian sources, and Fr Denis O'Sullivan of Monasterevin for his time and for drawing my attention to important primary sources. I am most grateful to Jennifer Montagu, Peter Humfrey, Deborah Howard, Damien Nelis, Andrew Smith. Finally, my gratitude to Monasterevin Community Council and Trinity College Trust Fund, who assisted with funding.

ENDNOTES

[1] Church of Sts Peter and Paul, Registry of Baptism, 29 August 1847, 'The first stone of the C. Church of Monasterevin was laid by the V. Revd. Doctor Haly August 26 1840, and the first mass celebrated therein on the 29 August 1847 – deo Gratis'. See NLI microfilm no. 4203 for a copy of the registry.

[2] A.M. Stewart and C. de Courcy, *Royal Hibernian Academy of Arts: Index of Exhibitors and Their Works 1826-1979* (London 1985) 106.

[3] T. Lacy, *Sights and Scenes in our Fatherland* (Wexford 1863) 184.

[4] Published in 1901 by Burns & Oates Ltd, 28 Orchard Street, London. Thanks to Fr Denis O'Sullivan for drawing my attention to this book.

[5] F.J. Kirk, *Some Notable Conversions in the county of Wexford* (London 1901) 15-16.

[6] These photographs are now in the possession of Michael Fitzpatrick, who has kindly given me permission to reproduce them here.

[7] D. Walsh, *100 Wexford Country Houses* (Wexford 1996) 83.

[8] The Auction Report in *The Watchman* of 26 November 1870 lists all 45 lots.

[9] A. Kavanagh and R. Murphy, *The Wexford Gentry* (Wexford 1994) 193.

[10] E. Ryan, *Monasterevin Parish: Some Historical Notes* (Naas 1958).

[11] W.E. Vaughan, *Sin, Sheep and Scotsmen: John George Adair and the Derryveagh evictions 1861* (Belfast 1983) 51-2.

[12] *Leinster Leader*, 4 Sept 1880, 2, available in diocesan archives, Carlow, manuscript number MCD/1880/02.

[13] F.J. Kirk, *Some Notable Conversions in the County of Wexford* (London 1901) 25.

[14] G. Lorenzetti, *Venice and its Lagoon: Historical and Artistic Guide*, translated by J. Guthrie (Trieste (1926) 1975) 508-9. Similar information on the architecture of S. Stefano is found in D. Howard, *Architectural History of Venice* (London 1980) 76, and in E. Concina, *A History of Venetian Architecture*, translated by J. Landry (Cambridge 1998) 109.

[15] I. Hogate, 'The Early History of Antonio Vivaries' "St. Jerome Altar Piece" and the beginning of the Renaissance Style in Venice', *The Burlington Magazine*, cxliii, 1174, January 2001, 21.

[16] Lorenzetti, *Venice and its Lagoon*, 509-11.

[17] F. Apollonio, *La Chiesa e il convento di S. Stefano in Venezia* (Venice 1911) 24. I am indebted to Dr Jennifer Montagu and Dr Victoria Avery for drawing my attention to this book.

[18] F. Apollonio, *La Chiesa e il convento di S. Stefano in Venezia* (Venice 1911) 27.

[19] Biblioteca del Museo Civico Correr, Venice, MS Cicogna no. 1877. Dr Avery kindly photo-copied the relevant sections of the manuscript.

[20] I would argue that the name given in the written sources and on the inscription, Corniani, is the correct one, though it has been suggested that the name might be Cornelius, the Latin form of the Venetian Cornaro. There is no evidence to support such an assumption and no reason to assume that the Cornaro family were involved. Cornaro and Corniani were two different families, and it was a member of the Corniani who commissioned the altar rails.

[21] Istituto dell Enciclopedia Italiana, *Dizionario Biografico degli Italiani*, xxix (Rome 1983) 271-3.

[22] The Corbelli family renewed the altar of St Nicholas of Tolento (the third altar in the left nave) from 1704 to 1709. The altar of the Annunciate (the second altar in the left nave) was renewed 'with marbles' from 1708, and from 1709 the Congregation of St Anne renewed 'with rich marbles' the first altar in the left nave. M.A. Chiari Moretto Wiel, 'La Chiesa di Santo Stefano: Il patrimonio artistico' in *Gli Agostiniani a Venezia e le Chiesa di S. Stefano* (Venice 1995) 275-7. Much of the information in Chiari's article comes from Agostino Nicolai's manuscript account on the church. My thanks to Prof Peter Humfrey for sending me the relevant sections from Chiari's chapter.

[23] Private correspondence with Dr Avery. I am indebted to Dr Avery for visiting the church of S. Stefano, and noticing the stylistic link between the altar rails and the Altar of Sta Monica, and for sending me the photographs of the altar. The Altar of Sta Monica was commissioned by Fr Giovanni Stefano Facchinelli, and is discussed in both the manuscript account of the church and in Apollonio, *La Chiesa e il convento di S. Stefano in Venezia* (Venice 1911) 12-13.

[24] M.A. Chiari Moretto Weil, A. Gallo and E. Merkel, *Chiesa di Santo Stefano: arte e devozione* (Venice 1996) 48-9.

[25] C. Semenzato, *La Scultura Veneta del Seicento e del Settecento* (Venice 1966) 26-7; C. Semenzato, 'Giovanni Comin' in J. Turner (ed.), *The Dictionary of Art* (London 1996) 650.

[26] Private correspondence with Dr Montagu.

[27] The possibility of Orazio Marinalli was suggested to me by Dr Avery in correspondence.

[28] A.E.P. Sanchez, 'Jossé de Corte' in Turner (ed.), *The Dictionary of Art*, 900.

[29] Apollonio, *La Chiesa di S. Stefano*, 52.

1 – A detail of the Hall of the Four Winds today
showing two of the four lower-level niches in which the bronze figures originally stood

Two figures of Aeolus at Powerscourt, county Wicklow

PATRICK BOWE

THE RESTORATION OF THE GREAT GROTTO IN THE GARDEN OF THE VILLA LITTA AT Lainate, near Milan, in Italy has shed new light on two bronze figures representing Aeolus, the God of the Winds, in the garden at Powerscourt, county Wicklow. The construction of the grotto at Lainate was begun in 1580 and was only completed ten years later.[1] It was ordered by Pirro Borromeo-Visconti (who is known as Pirro I), in whose family the estate had been for many years. The university-educated Pirro became advisor to the Dukes of Mantua. He had already been ennobled by Philip II of Spain, when, at the age of 20, he began the grotto's construction.

Pirro employed the architect Martino Bassi (1541-1591), who had been involved with the reconstruction of the cathedral in Milan, to design the grotto, or *nymphaeum*, as it was sometimes called. Integral to the design of the grotto was a complex series of waterworks – fountains, pools, water jets and sprays, including water-jokes, called *giochi d'acqua*, in which visitors to the grotto would be squirted unexpectedly by jets and sprays at various points during their tour. The hydraulics engineer who was commissioned to design these water effects was Agostino Ramelli (1531-1608). He installed nearly a mile of pipes to carry water from a twenty-metre-high water-tower into the many different rooms which still make up the grotto.

The grotto rooms housed the great art treasures collected by Pirro, including Leonardo's *Madonna Litta*, together with paintings by Bronzino, Correggio, Bernardino Luini, and others. Also in the collection were sculptures such as the figure of Venus (now known as the Mellon Venus) and another of Bacchus (both in the National Gallery in Washington). Recent studies by the art historian Alessandro Morandotti attribute them to the sculptor Francesco Brambilla the Younger (1530-1599). In addition to the artworks, the rooms also contained a collection of fossils, minerals, archaeological fragments, coins, holy relics, and other curious items to make up what was to be known later as a 'cabinet of curiosities'.

The centrepiece of the grotto building is a rotunda called the Hall of the Four Winds (Plates 1, 2). It is actually an octagon, lit from open porches at its northern and southern ends and from a high-level lantern twenty metres above the floor level. Beneath this lantern extends a ceiling with a balustraded colonnade painted in *trompe l'oeil* against a blue sky. The lower or middle level of the rotunda (octagon) is decorated with *rocaille*, or ornamental rockwork, which is studded with decorative patterns of mother-of-pearl. Niches frame statues of the four seasons, as well as figures of Venus and Mercury. The rich and crowded effect is completed at ground level with a further series of rockwork niches. Four of these were originally filled by bronze figures representing the four winds, which gave the hall its name. (These figures were later referred to in some sources as figures of Aeolus, the God of the Winds.) In his recent studies, Morandotti has attributed all of the figures in the hall to Francesco Brambilla the Younger, who had previously worked on the reconstruction of Milan cathedral with Martino Bassi. The designs for the vault decorations, carried out in patterns of black and white pebbles which divide the rockwork niches, are attributed to the painter, Camillo Procacini (1550-1625), who is principally known as a painter, in his early days, of religious works.

Much of the original collection of art works has been dispersed, although the history of the dispersal has not yet been studied in detail. However, it is known that the figures representing the Four Winds were purchased by Prince Jerome Napoleon, a first cousin of the emperor Napoleon III of France, and, like him, a nephew of the emperor Napoleon I. Prince Jerome Napoleon placed two of the figures in the great greenhouse at his country chateau of Prangins. The other two he placed as indoor fountain figures in the Palais Royal in Paris. One of the latter two figures was located in one of the state rooms, and the other on a staircase.[2] Prince Jerome Napoleon wrote of his purchase of the figures, his placement of them at Prangins and in the Palais Royal, and his later disposal of them, in a letter dated 2 July 1874:

> The two statues come from the property of the Duke of Litta at Milan, where they were placed in the country at Lainate. I bought four there, two belong to Mr. Lucas, to whom I sold my chateau here. They are in a great greenhouse. The figures should be placed against a wall, I cannot do a drawing, not having the dimensions. At the Palais Royal, the figures of Aeolus spewed gas from their mouths and water from under their arms, it was original and beautiful. The statues are from the 17th century, a little baroque, but, well placed in a garden, in a greenhouse or on a staircase, they would have a good effect.[3]

After the Franco-German War of 1870-71, the Palais Royal was burned by the Communards, in May 1871.[4] The two figures of Aeolus were saved from the conflagration. Subsequently, the whole of Prince Napoleon's collections were sent to London and sold at Christie's on Thursday 9 May 1872 and following days. The two figures of Aeolus were purchased by Lord Powerscourt through Mr Agnew.[5]

2 – A cross-section of the Hall of the Four Winds from a preliminary drawing by the Milanese architect and furniture designer Giuseppe Levati. He was responsible at the end of the eighteenth century for the restoration / reconstruction of the grotto or nymphaeum. The figures of the Four Winds are still in position in their ground-floor niches at that time.

3 – A plate from THE HISTORY AND DESCRIPTION OF POWERSCOURT, *written by the 7th Viscount Powerscourt, showing the Triton Fountain, with the bronze figures of Aeolus in their new position.*

Lord Powerscourt wrote of the figures in his *History and Description of Powerscourt*, published in 1903:

> I was anxious that works of art of such importance should be placed in a prominent position, and made inquiries from various friends, among others from Mr. Brinsley Marlay, well known as a connoisseur of Italian art, as to who should be consulted. He mentioned that there was no better authority than Mr. Francis Cranmer Penrose, at that time architect to the Chapter of St. Paul's Cathedral, London. I therefore asked Mr. Penrose to come over and view the site, and suggested to him the idea of a classical composition, such as may be seen in several country places in England, and notably at Versailles, at La Granja, near Madrid, and elsewhere, with a perron with a central recess or alcove, in which the figures of Aeolus should be the salient features. I had seen many examples of a similar character at Rome and other places. Mr. Penrose took up the idea with his characteristic zest. And the result was a design which he carried out, placing these grand statues in the centre, spouting water into a stone basin, with a pediment surmounting them, in the arch of which is placed a head of Apollo, the God of the Sun, with a sundial beneath it, between the two statues, the gnomon of which is constructed of bronze, like the figures, with the well-known motto, Horas non numero nisi serenas.[6]

In his book, Lord Powerscourt continues his description of the perron and its immediate setting (Plate 3). He states that it was his intention to arrange that all the garden urns and statuary in that section of the garden would be in bronze to reflect the bronze materials of which the Aeolus figures (which he sometimes describes as 'Triton' figures) were made (Plate 4).[7]

4 – A late nineteenth-century photograph showing the bronze figures and their then new setting in the overall context of the garden at Powerscourt (courtesy National Library of Ireland)

For the first time, it is now possible not only to view the figures of Aeolus in their setting in the garden at Powerscourt, but also to envision them in the setting for which they were originally executed – the Hall of the Four Winds in the grotto of the Villa Litta at Lainate.[8]

———

ACKNOWLEDGEMENTS

Dr Viviana Croci and Enrico Benzo of the Associazione 'Amici di Villa Litta' Lainate, and Dr Alessandro Morandotti.

ENDNOTES

[1]   See Georgina Masson, *Italian Gardens* (London and New York 1961); Associazione Amici di Villa Litta di Lainate, *Villa Borromeo Visconti Litta Lainate* (Lainate, n.d.).

[2]   That the other two figures were placed as ornaments in the greenhouse at the Chateau de Prangins can be assumed from a letter written by Prince Jerome Napoleon from the Chateau of Prangins and quoted later in the article. The author has not been able to ascertain if they are still in position there.

[3]   The letter was written by the prince to Emile Ollivier, who was President of the Chambre des Deputies under the emperor Napoleon III. A copy was passed to Mr Delane, the editor of *The Times*, who passed it on to his acquaintance, Lord Powerscourt. See 7th Viscount Powerscourt, *A History and Description of Powerscourt* (1903) 83.

[4]   The Communards were the adherents of the Commune, which was a government established on communistic principles in Paris during 1871.

[5]   Mr Agnew was presumably a principal of the London-based fine-art dealership today known as Agnews.

[6]   Powerscourt, *History and Description*, 85. Brinsley Marlay was the owner of Belvedere House, county Westmeath, where he constructed a series of garden terraces with balustrades based on those in the Old English style at Haddon Hall, Derbyshire. The term 'perron', used by Lord Powerscourt to refer to the architectural setting constructed for the Aeolus figures, is normally used to refer to a platform, ascended by steps in front of a church or mansion and upon which the doors open. It is sometimes applied to a double flight of steps ascending to such a door.

[7]   For example, Powerscourt describes his acquisition, for nearby locations in the garden, of two fine bronze groups representing children, by Morin, a contemporary of Clodion. He also describes his purchase in St Petersburg of two bronze vases belonging to the architect of St Isaac's cathedral in that city.

[8]   The grotto was restored in the eighteenth century by a descendant of Pirro Borromeo-Visconti, called Pompeo Litta, after which the villa became known as the Villa Borromeo Visconti Litta. The architect employed by Litta was Giuseppe Levati. In 1970 the villa and its grotto came into the hands of the municipality of Lainate. Now, with the assistance of the Association of the Friends of the Villa Litta Lainate, a new and handsome restoration has been carried out.

Bridge House, Kilkenny: tracing the history of a building

JANE FENLON

K ILKENNY IS GENERALLY REGARDED AS ONE OF THE BEST, IF NOT THE BEST PRE-served, medieval towns in Ireland. Obvious reminders of the past glories of the town may be seen in many of the larger buildings that still remain standing – the castle, the churches, and on a more domestic scale, Rothe House and the Shee Alms House. However, behind bland eighteenth and nineteenth-century façades, remnants of the many substantial early stone houses enumerated in the Ormonde Rentals and other seventeenth-century documents may still be found. The purpose of this article is to outline the history of the building at Nos 88-89 John Street, generally known as Bridge House. It is not intended to be an exhaustive study; rather it seeks to explore various aspects of the building's appearance through documents, maps and illustrations. Emphasis will be placed on establishing a chronology of the buildings on the site from the sixteenth century, its transforma-tion, and its context within the overall development of the town.

Bridge House stands on the east bank of the River Nore adjoining St John's Bridge in Kilkenny (Plate 1).[1] The building, well known because of its distinctive double doorway and large three-storey bow, has often featured in views of Kilkenny Castle taken from beyond the bridge. The building has two storeys over a basement, with a large bow and late eighteenth-century façade at No. 89, while the façade of No. 88 is of a later date. A double entrance door was inserted in the nineteenth cen-tury to give access to both houses. No. 89 is situated closest to the river, with the orientation of both houses towards the street.

References to Bridge House may be found in any general discussion of Georgian architecture in Kilkenny.[2] However, behind the façade, under plaster-cov-ered walls and decorated ceilings, an earlier thick-walled structure forms the greater part of No. 89. An examination of the current floor plan of No. 89 reveals that the

1, 2 – North-west and west elevations of Bridge House, John's Street, Kilkenny, showing the prox-imity of the house to St John's Bridge and the River Nore (courtesy Blackwood Associates, Dublin)

earlier building had its gable towards the street, with other heavy stone structures on the east side (Plate 3). In other words, the long side of the earlier building was parallel to the river and there were various other early structures to the east (Plate 2). The later bow front on No. 89 has cloaked the front gable wall that would have faced the street, while the opposing gable, with remnants of early window opes, may still be seen from the rear of the building. In appearance, the street gable of the earlier house would have been similar, albeit on a larger scale, to that of the late sixteenth-century Shee Alms House, which is situated across the bridge in Rose Inn Street.

At this stage it may be useful to provide some background history to the site in an effort to establish some form of chronicle for the building. Bridge House is situated across the river from the old 'Hightown' and the castle. The site is close to a crossing place on the river, and a bridge was built nearby as early as 1223.[3] Further up John Street are the remains of St John's church, a fragment of the larger building that had belonged to the Augustinian Priory of St John founded by William Marshall in 1211. At the time of its dissolution in 1540 the priory had extensive outbuildings. St John's was granted, with part of its extensive land holdings, to the mayor and citizens of Kilkenny around 1541.[4] The lands 'in the area of St John's' granted to the Corporation of Kilkenny included a number of buildings described as 'Bake House, Infirmary, Cloister, Chapter House and Hospital'.[5] In the early 1660s when James Butler, 1st Duke of Ormonde, returned to Ireland after the restoration of Charles II to the throne of England, a dispute arose between the duke and the Corporation over the ownership of some houses and lands in Kilkenny. Because both ducal and Corporation lands had been seized by Cromwellian settlers there was a measure of uncertainty about leases. Handwritten lists of the disputed properties

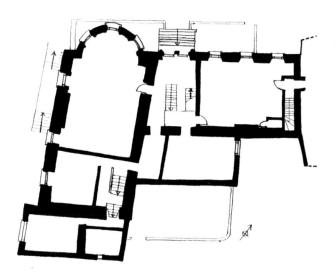

3 – Bridge House: ground-floor plan
(courtesy Blackwood Associates, Dublin)

exist, but these are not always easy to decipher, nor is it possible to identify all of the properties described in the documents.[6] The dispute was resolved in 1676; at that time Ormonde's half-brother, George Mathew (d.1724) obtained a 99-year lease on a property referred to as No. 91 in the Ormonde rental books. In later rentals the property at No. 91 is described as 'The decayed Stone House on the bridge wth another stone house thereunto belonging late the holding of Captain George Mathews', with the additional information that it was 'situate at the end of St John's Bridge south side and is the house wherein Counc[illor] Egan now lives in'.[7] The lease had changed hands again in 1722 when Councillor Derby Egan took over from Mathews, and, on the evidence available, the ground rent then continued to be held by heirs of the Egan family until the end of the 1840s.[8] The Ormonde Rentals provide evidence that the Ormondes were ground landlords throughout the eighteenth and nineteenth centuries, although there is no evidence for the commonly held belief that Charles Butler, Earl of Arran, had ever lived in the property.[9] By 1875, after the expiry of the period of a second 99-year lease, the Marquis of Ormonde was described as 'the immediate lessor'.[10] That this was indeed the site of Bridge House was confirmed by an entry in the Ormonde Rentals of 1830, where No. 91 was described as 'The decayed stone House on the bridge wth another stone house thereto belonging and a garden. This house is the next house to St John's Bridge on the right-hand side as you go over from Rose Inn Street to John Street, and is situated in John's Street where Lewis Anderson Esqr Sherriff of the city of Kilkenny lives March 4th 1830 EH.'[11] The leaseholder for the buildings on the site during the crucial years of the mid-eighteenth century, when major rebuilding took place, was Thomas Barnes, a Kilkenny-born lawyer working in Dublin.[12] It was Barnes who was responsible for the major remodelling of Bridge House which took place following the flood of 1763.

Of particular significance in the description of the house given in the lease of No. 91 is the reference to it being 'on the bridge wth another stone house thereunto'. This suggests that the house was in close proximity to or even an integral part of the bridge. There is evidence for a tower situated on the west side of the bridge, described as 'the bridge of St John's Castle'.[13] This 'castle' served as a gateway into Hightown, with a tall tower built above it. When the River Nore flooded in 1564 the bridge and 'castle' were damaged, and probably other buildings that were close to the river at that time. John Rocque's map of Kilkenny of 1758 (Plate 4) shows a bridge that may have been an early seventeenth-century rebuild, as the plan of the 'castle' was depicted on the west end where it was aligned with Rose Inn Street.[14] Bradley has made the suggestion that there may have been another gate on the opposite or east side of John's Bridge. This would seem a reasonable assumption, because he also tells us that 'the suburb of St John's functioned throughout the mid-

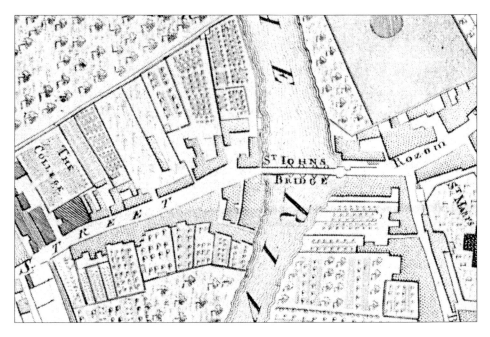

4 – Map of Kilkenny, 1758, by John Roque
(courtesy Board of Trinity College, Dublin)

dle ages as a separate ward with its own annually appointed provost who was responsible to the Sovereign of the Hightown for its administration'.[15] Town gateways such as those in the walled Hightown of Kilkenny served two functions: they could be closed for protection, and also used to collect tariffs from traffic passing through. Gateways in walled precincts were a feature of large religious establishments like that of St John's priory, where Bradley has identified two gatehouses and a suggested third, 'at the junction of John Street and John's bridge'.[16] The position on the river of the earlier building on the site of Bridge House, in such close proximity to the bridge, would suggest that it was built for a purpose linked to that structure.

Kilkenny city was a favoured subject for illustrators from the 1690s onwards. The earliest of these was Francis Place (1647-1728) from Dunsdale, near Durham in England, who visited Kilkenny *c.*1699, and, happily, several of his drawings of the city with its buildings have survived (Plates 6-8). The other early illustrator was Henry Pratt (fl.1695-1708), a mapmaker who published a panorama of 'The City of Kilkenny' in 1708. Rocque's map provides a basis for understanding some of these early illustrations of the town. For instance, on his map the footprint of the earlier building within No. 89 was depicted without a bow, and the street elevation was aligned with the south side of the bridge in 1758. Also shown on the map was the position of Bridge House relative to Kilkenny College and the square tower/gate that was called the Castle of St John's Bridge. Questions always need to be asked regarding the topographical correctness of any illustrator's work, and about the inaccuracy, or otherwise, when studying their depictions of buildings. In this case, however, by using Rocque's map combined with local knowledge when comparing these two illustrator's work, some shadowy images have emerged for the earlier buildings on the site of Bridge House at the turn of the seventeenth century.

At first glance the Pratt illustration might be dismissed as fanciful. However, on closer examination it may be seen that several features that appear on it are also depicted on the more accomplished and detailed drawings by Francis Place of 1699. The aim of the Pratt illustration would seem to be more in the way of a catalogue of the principal buildings of Kilkenny city rather than any attempt to provide an accurate topographical representation of the city (Plate 5). The key at the foot of the drawing would seem to confirm that this was so.

Although the artists have taken their renditions from different viewpoints, comparison may be made between the appearance and location of the principal buildings. Place took as his viewpoint Wind Gap Hill, a height (although somewhat exaggerated) beyond the point where present-day Maudlin Street meets the Dublin

5 – Henry Pratt, THE CITY OF KILKENNY
(courtesy National Library of Ireland)

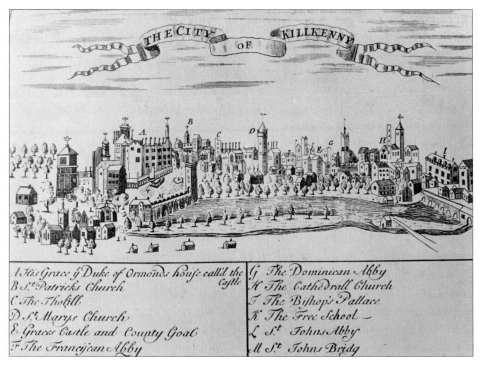

A His Grace ÿ Duke of Ormonds house call'd the Castle
B St Patricks Church
C The Tholfill
D St Marys Church
E Graces Castle and County Goal
F The Francijcan Abby
G The Dominican Abby
H The Cathedrall Church
I The Bishop's Pallace
K The Free School
L St Johns Abby
M St Johns Bridg

Road (Plate 6), while Pratt used a bird's-eye view taken from an imaginary point between Green's Bridge and St John's Bridge. Kilkenny Castle is probably the most prominent starting point, and while Pratt's drawing of that group of buildings is awkward and often out of scale, it does include most of the components that Place uses. These include six tall chimneys on the main residential block, ancillary buildings, raised terrace, and the small banqueting house with its classical peristyle (Plates 5, 7). At the other end of the town, St Canice's Cathedral and the cap-less round tower, with the Archbishop's Palace to the east, may be seen in both views. The lantern on the tholsel, with St Mary's church, occupy the central space, and the ruined St John's Priory, marked L in Pratt's panorama, is elegantly drawn by Place. Kilkenny College, the old building, may also be seen in both images. Pratt's view of the college building, marked K, shows it situated to the east and slightly south of St John's Bridge, while Place depicts it closing the end of the view down Maudlin Street. The position of the school is reasonably accurate in both drawings. Overall it could be said, based on Place's drawings and on Rocque's map, that Pratt's buildings and topographical positioning were not all that fanciful.

To return to Bridge House, in the Pratt drawing St John's Bridge is clearly marked M. On the west end can be seen a tall tower, representing the tower of St John's Bridge Gate, while on the east side, seemingly part of the bridge, a tall house with two chimneys and a projecting central bay is illustrated on the site of the present Bridge House. Place also has a house in this position, but it is insubstantial in the finished work, and we must go to his preparatory drawings of the area in order to clarify details of these buildings.

In one of a series of preparatory sketches carried out by Place for his finished drawing of Kilkenny may be seen (as in the Pratt drawing) St Mary's church, the

6 – Francis Place, a view of Kilkenny from Wind Gap Hill
(*courtesy National Gallery of Ireland*)

7 – Francis Place, north elevation of Kilkenny Castle
(courtesy National Gallery of Ireland)

tholsel, the Magdalen gate and Kilkenny College (Plate 8). Also in this drawing the tower/gate on St John's Bridge is depicted as a tall tower with three windows, one above the other, on each of two elevations, the east side shadowed in dark wash. St Mary's church is visible in the group of foreshortened buildings similar to that shown in the Pratt illustration. In front of the tower/gate, Place has drawn a building with a pointed gable on the east side, with another building attached to the south gable and a smaller lower building to the east of it. I would suggest that in this drawing Place has provided a sketch of the form of the buildings that were on the site of Bridge House in 1699.

Further verification that Place and Pratt were reasonably accurate in their representation and placing of buildings may be confirmed by details in another illustration of the area. Kilkenny College, as illustrated by Place and Pratt, may be compared with the same building which features in an oil painting of about 1757, attributed to Thomas Mitchell (1735-1790) (Plate 9). In this work the college building may be seen just to the left of the Maudlin gate and tower, where it is shown with two gables to the south and three to the east elevation. This painting is said to have been in the collection of the Marquis of Ormonde in 1850, and 'that it was painted in oil about eighty or ninety years back'.[17] A more detailed drawing of the college, taken from the painting attributed to Mitchell, is provided in a lithograph of

8 – Francis Place, preparatory drawing of a view of Kilkenny from Wind Gap Hill, 1699

The buildings on the site of Bridge House are on the left, with the 'castle' of the bridge and St Mary's church rising
up behind them. (courtesy Museum of Art, Rhode Island School of Design)

9 – Thomas Mitchell (attrib.), A VIEW OF KILKENNY, c.1757 (courtesy NGI)

that drawing by the Rev James Graves, the eminent Kilkenny antiquarian who identified it as being 'the Old Kilkenny School'.[18]

The position of St John's Bridge over the River Nore was crucial to the development of Bridge House. The alignment of the structure was sometimes altered when it was being renewed through the centuries. St John's Bridge is known to have been destroyed by flood in 1564, but a definite date for rebuilding the bridge has not been discovered. There was a bridge referred to as St John's Bridge in 1707, illustrated by Pratt in 1708, and it also appeared on Roque's map of 1758. That particular bridge, which was aligned with Rose Inn Street, was eventually destroyed by flood in 1763, when widespread damage was also reported in the area. Following the flood it seems that the Corporation took a decision to make good use of the opportunity afforded by erecting two fine bridges with handsome classical details over the River Nore, on adjacent sites to the earlier Green's Bridge and St John's Bridge. When the new St John's Bridge was built after 1763, the structure was not aligned with Rose Inn Street, but was moved northwards along the Horse Slip. This allowed the approaches to the bridge to be widened on the east side. On Ordnance Survey maps of 1841-42 the entrance to John Street was shown as wide and expansive, providing a suitable situation for an important house.[19] This additional space would have allowed plenty of room for the insertion of the bow and a projection, probably a set of wide steps, that appear on the 1841 map. In Griffith's Valuation of 1850 there were two houses on the site at 88-89 John's Street, and these were valued as greater than £20 each for rateable purposes.[20]

Within the houses there is evidence of major alterations to the structures at different periods. In No. 89 the roof height was increased using red-brick walls, chimneys were moved, a bow was added, the floors raised, and decorative plasterwork installed. Additions were also added to the rear, and a front façade was constructed, apparently in two phases – the first phase being coeval with the bow, the second when an additional storey was added and the double doorway inserted sometime after 1820 (Plate 10). The style of the first phase of alterations is suitable to a date c.1770. The 1763 flood had probably caused considerable damage to the building on the site – at least flooding of the basement areas and perhaps even some structural injury, if, as suggested, the house was attached to the bridge in some way. The new St John's Bridge was not completed until 1782 when the palisade was finally added.[21]

In conclusion, I would suggest that the original structure on the site of Bridge House had been one of the ancillary buildings of the Priory of St John. A building on the site was described as decayed in the seventeenth century, which would indicate that it was at least of sixteenth-century date. With the dissolution of the monasteries, when church properties were granted to Kilkenny Corporation, some of these may not have been inhabited immediately and so fell further into decay. Then in the

10 – R Gibbs, Kilkenny Castle, c.1820, showing Bridge House to the left of St John's Bridge.

No. 89 is seen to be freestanding, at least on the upper storey. Other illustrations of the time, such as J.E. Neale's lithograph KILKENNY BRIDGE AND CASTLE (1819), confirm that this was so. (courtesy Kilkenny Archaeological Society)

latter half of the seventeenth century there was the dispute between the Duke of Ormonde and the Corporation over ownership of properties that had continued from 1660 to 1676. Following the resolution of that dispute and the change of tenant, there may have been some rebuilding/restoration carried out. The major repair/ rebuilding work, which included the addition of the bow, was put in place after the 1763 flood. The appearance of the building now called Bridge House is essentially Georgian in style, and these changes may be dated to two phases of work probably carried out from the 1770s onwards. Within the context of buildings in the town, Bridge House could be compared with Butler House – the dower house of the Ormonde family that was also remodelled about the same time. These houses appear to have been the only two examples in the town at that time with large curved bays. Those on Butler House are on the rear elevation of the building.

Although some of the problems concerning Bridge House have been addressed in this essay, more questions remain to be answered. For instance, did the early building on the site of Bridge House originally form an integral part of one of the bridges? Ironically, when St John's Bridge was replaced in 1910 it was again aligned with Rose Inn Street, thus creating the rather cramped position for Bridge House that exists today.

ACKNOWLEDGEMENTS

I would like to thank Blackwood Associates Architects for their generous assistance with the plan and photographs for this article. I am grateful to John Kirwan and Margery Brady for information quoted in endnotes 8 and 10 respectively, and also Kilkenny Court Hotel. Special thanks to Angela Murphy, *Irish Historic Town Atlas*, RIA; the staff at the Tholsel, Kilkenny; National Archives; Manuscripts Department, National Library of Ireland. Freddie O'Dwyer of Dúchas has provided information on Thomas Barnes (note 12) and Conleth Manning, also of Dúchas, drew my attention to the seventeenth-century date for the rebuilding of the bridge (note 14). Finally, I would like to acknowledge and thank Donal Fenlon for his assistance with background research for this article.

ENDNOTES

[1] Although the bridge is now called John's Bridge, it was known as St John's Bridge, and for the sake of consistency this is the form that has been used throughout this article.

[2] P. Smithwick, 'Georgian Kilkenny', *Bulletin of the Irish Georgian Society*, iv, 4, (1963) 93; K.M. Lanigan and G. Tyler, *Kilkenny: Its Architecture and History* (Belfast 1987) 97.

[3] J. Bradley, *Kilkenny, Irish Historic Towns Atlas* (Dublin 2000) 21.

[4] *ibid.*, 13.

[5] NLI, Ormonde Papers, Ms 11,934.

[6] *ibid.*, also Ms 11,048/36,7,8.

[7] *ibid.*, Ms 7864.

[8] *ibid.*, Ms 23,790-797, Ms 11,048. Kilkenny Castle, document no. 72 from the collection at Kilkenny Castle, catalogued by John Kirwan. In the Ormonde Rentals from 1722 to the 1840s the same description of the house is repeated and the tenant's name throughout is Derby Egan.

[9] Some of the Ormonde Rentals were transferred into the Earl of Arran's name by his brother, the 2nd Duke of Ormonde, and this may be the basis for the misunderstanding.

[10] Valuation Office Dublin, Lessors of Bridge House, Kilkenny, post 1875.

[11] NLI, Ormonde Papers, Ms 25,027; list of rentals 1830/31, descriptions copied with annotations.

[12] Barnes features as a character of that name in Sir Walter Scott's novel *Guy Mannering*. The novel, although located in Scotland, is based on the famous Annesley court case of the 1740s. In it Barnes features as a valet.

[13] NLI, Ormonde Papers, Ms 11,934.

[14] NLI, Ms D3620b (Ormonde Collection), Blake Butler Transcripts, Tithes of Corporation, 'To the masons for building St John's Bridge...', 1618-19

[15] Bradley, *Kilkenny, Irish Historic Towns Atlas*, 4.

[16] *ibid.*

[17] J. Browne, 'Kilkenny College', *JRSAI*, vol. i, no. 1 (1849-51) 221-9.

[18] *ibid.*, plate facing page 229.

[19] National Archives, Dublin, Ordnance Survey maps, Kilkenny 1841 (Kilkenny *c.*1842).

[20] Bradley, *Kilkenny, Irish Historic Towns Atlas*, map 8.

[21] Kilkenny Corporation minute books 1763-1782.

Building empires: architecture, politics and the Board of Works 1760-1860

FREDERICK O'DWYER

T HE HISTORY OF THE IRISH BOARD OF WORKS CAN PERHAPS BE TRACED BACK AS far as the Norman invasion. It is not proposed to attempt that task here, but rather to examine the development of public works architecture after 1600, with particular emphasis on the period from 1760 to 1860 and the various legislative changes that occurred during that time. This legislation provided the context for the major building programmes of the Victorian and Edwardian eras, and remained in place after the foundation of the new state.[1]

The start date of 1760 marks the mid-point in a period of major reorganisation that saw, *inter alia*, the abolition of the Office of Surveyor General, the sideways move (effectively a demotion) of its incumbent Thomas Eyre (1708-1772) to the post of Chief Engineer of the Ordnance, and the establishment of a board of works to take over some of his duties. The concluding date of 1860, as well as being a neat century ahead, marks a period of change both in personnel and in duties within the Board of Public Works following the retirement of Jacob Owen (1778-1870), arguably the major figure of nineteenth-century public works architecture in Ireland.

There have been a number of significant publications in recent years on eighteenth-century developments. These have been notably (in order of publication) Murray Fraser's 'Public building and colonial policy in Dublin, 1760-1800' (in *Architectural History*, 1985)[2] and two works by Edward McParland: 'The surveyor general in Ireland in the eighteenth century' (in *Architectural History*, 1995)[3] and *Public Architecture in Ireland 1680-1760* (Yale 2001). While in terms of dates McParland and Fraser might appear to dovetail, it should be noted that Fraser's areas of discussion were the civic improvements of the Wide Streets Commissioners and the building of the Custom House by the Revenue Board, rather than the operations of the public works departments of central government – the area given greatest scope in the two McParland publications. It should also be noted that James Gandon (1742-1823) (the subject of an earlier monograph by McParland),[4] who designed not just the Custom House, but the Four Courts, the King's Inns, and extensions to the Parliament House, never held office under the Board of Works.

SEVENTEENTH AND EIGHTEENTH CENTURIES

Early in the seventeenth century an important reorganisation of Irish public works took place. This was the granting of a royal patent in 1613 to Sir Josias Bodley, creating him Director-General and Overseer of the Fortifications and Buildings in Ireland. This was an amalgamation of Bodley's former office, Superintendent of the Castles, with that of the Supervision of the Royal Works.[5] Royal works, in the Irish context, concerned royal or vice-regal residences, primarily Dublin Castle, and could be described as the civil as opposed to the military side of public works. The amalgamation was completed with the death of the last clerk of the Royal Works in 1625. The title of the office changed twice before it was finally settled, in 1670, as Surveyor General of the Fortifications and Buildings, William Robinson (c.1642-1712) (architect of the Royal Hospital Kilmainham) being the first to occupy the post, which was held by patent.[6] Up until 1700, royal palaces and other public buildings remained the responsibility of the king's government, to be built, maintained and paid for without reference to Parliament. Following the defeat of the Jacobite forces in 1691, a decision was taken to accommodate soldiers in barracks around the country, in readiness for any revolt.[7] This saw the passing of an Act in the Irish parliament in 1697 (9 Wm III c.4, I.), granting £25,000 (raised from tobacco duties) for the building of barracks, and, in 1700-01, the creation by Parliament of two bodies with responsibility for barracks. These were the Trustees of Barracks, a property-holding body, and the Overseers of Barracks (commonly known as the Barrack Board), responsible for the erection and maintenance of barracks. This pioneering scheme, which for long had no English equivalent, was a parliamentary innovation, and as such was within the jurisdiction of the (Irish) House of Commons, who voted the funds. The most obvious choice of architect for these works was the Surveyor General. Robinson's immediate successors, Thomas Burgh (1700-30) and Edward Lovett Pearce (1731-33), are perhaps the best-known holders of the post, both being associated with the development of classical architecture in Ireland. Burgh's major building in Dublin was the Royal (now Collins) Barracks (1703-25), while Pearce's masterly Parliament House (begun 1728) was of European significance.[8]

Pearce's successors, the last three surveyors general, are less well known:

2 – Anon., pastel of Captain Thomas Eyre (1750)

After a military career in Georgia and South Carolina, Eyre retired with the rank of captain while serving as an engineer on Rattan – an island off Honduras – in 1752. He returned to Ireland to take up the post of Surveyor and Engineer General. (courtesy Christie's)

Arthur Dobbs (1734-44), Arthur Jones Nevill (1744-52) and Thomas Eyre (1752-62). All the surveyors general held parliamentary seats at some time in their careers, though this was not a prerequisite for the job. As McParland notes in his most recent work, there has been a tendency to regard these three as sinecurists rather than as professional architects or engineers. In reassessing their roles, he elevates Nevill (c.1712-1771) and Eyre to the professions while apparently leaving Dobbs (1689-1765) as a placeman, though he also notes, ambiguously, 'in the absence of evidence to the contrary ... it is reasonable to attribute to individual surveyors general the works, in the castle and elsewhere, for which their estimates and payments to them are recorded'.[9] It seems that the strongest professional case can be made for Eyre, who, as he states, had a background in military engineering in the American colonies (Plate 2).[10] He also had a notable architectural pedigree: his grandfather, Colonel John Eyre, was the builder of Eyrecourt Castle in east Galway, one of the earliest classical houses in Ireland.

While the Barrack Board was responsible to Parliament, the Surveyor General was not, being an officer under the crown. This caused difficulties and friction, and indeed had led to Nevill's departure and his expulsion from the Commons.[11] Robinson had been jailed in 1703 and declared unfit for any public office over alleged misrepresentation in his capacity as Deputy Receiver-General. In

3 – Detail of the patent issued to the Barrack Board in 1759

The vignette and arms are those of King George II.
(courtesy National Archives)

1709 a Commons committee enquiring into the state of the Parliament House found that he had also received money for maintenance that had not been carried out.[12] After various unsuccessful attempts to bring the Surveyor General under official control, in 1759 a new Barrack Board, in the form of a body of salaried commissioners, was established, which was to have responsibilities of some kind for all government building in Ireland (Plate 3);[13] that is, in addition to retaining the responsibility for building and maintaining barracks, the Board assumed responsibility for supervising costs and for the execution of Ordnance and public buildings. There were seven commissioners: Henry Loftus, Henry Lyons, John Magill, Carleton Whitelocke, Henry Sandford, Thomas Adderley and Robert Cunninghame. All but Whitelocke were members of Parliament. The new Board got off to a quick start, publishing in 1760 a comprehensive schedule of dilapidations for every barrack in the country, co-authored by Lyons, Magill, Adderley and Whitelocke.[14] Magill (1703-1775) was the rising man. According to an anonymous tract of the time, which dubbed him 'Buttermilk Jack', Magill was a former journeyman carpenter and sometime theatrical clown turned valuer and surveyor, the son of a carpenter and a buttermilk vendor in Dublin's Clarendon Market.[15] He had previously served as Dobbs's deputy and, if the tract is to believed, had worked for Pearce on the Parliament House before that. In 1747, two years after his election as an MP for the borough of Rathcormack (allegedly bought for £500), he had been a member of a committee that reported on the state of the Parliament House. In business, he was associated with the Gardiner estate, owning a sandpit on Sackville Street and some of the 'footlots' – parcels of reclaimed land – in the North Strand area where he lived.[16] The sandpit must have been particularly lucrative: it appears as a gap on the otherwise built-up street on Roque's map (1756) and was not developed until after 1769.

There was not, however, universal agreement about the new Board's terms of reference. The Master of the Ordnance, the Earl of Kildare, wishing to keep fortifications under the control of his department, had these removed from the Barrack Board's limited supervisory remit in 1761. With the formal suppression of the Office of Surveyor General in 1762,[17] the transformation of the Barrack Board was complete, the Earl of Halifax, the Lord Lieutenant, conferring on the Barrack Board the powers of a board of works.[18] By this was meant that to the administrative function of the Barrack Board had been added the executive function of constructing and maintaining buildings. This solved the problem of dual departmental administration between the old Barrack Board and the Surveyor General's office, the new Board being able to direct its own works. The initial operational relationship between the administrative and executive sides of the Barrack Board is unclear, though details emerge in later documents of the arrangements made after the passing of further legislation in the 1790s.

In his chronicle of change, McParland sets the date for the legal termination of Eyre's appointment as Surveyor General as a king's letter of 11 August 1762, coming into effect with the revocation of his patent on 9 May 1763, the year in which, he states, the English architect Henry Keene (1726-1776) 'first appears as architect to the (Barrack) Board'.[19] Keene and his associate John Sanderson had drawn the (working) plans and elevations for the West Front of Trinity College, Dublin (built 1752-59), which had been designed by the London merchant and amateur architect Theodore Jacobsen.[20] It is clear from a number of sources, however, that Eyre was doomed once Halifax, the new lord lieutenant, arrived in Dublin in early October 1761, over eighteen months before the revocation of the patent. According to Howard Colvin, citing a contemporary source, 'in 1761 Keene was taken to Ireland [by Halifax] and ... in the following year was "appointed by him Architect of the Kingdom of Ireland for His Majesty's Works there" '.[21] On the face of it, Keene, who later designed a church for Halifax on his Sussex estates, was the

Lord Lieutenant's protégé. No doubt Keene was happy to be regarded as such, but, as we shall see, Keene's nomination may have come from a different quarter entirely.

From Eyre's own letters of 25 December 1761 and 12 January 1762 (to the Chief Secretary, William Gerard Hamilton, and Speaker Ponsonby respectively), it is clear that his removal from the post of Surveyor General was discussed at a meeting he attended in Dublin Castle on 20 December, at which he sought compensation for loss of office. While his surveyor-general patent was not revoked for some time, his new patent, in the subordinate role of Chief Engineer of the Ordnance, ran from 1 January 1762, and it would appear that from this date he was effectively out of office. This is confirmed by his account book, which shows that he received no funds for works in the calendar year 1762.[22] When Eyre was eventually granted a pension in 1764 (for £200 rather than the £300-plus sought), the explanatory statement in the Commons Journal stated that his post had been suppressed in 1761.[23] Among the perquisites he lost was his dwelling house and office in the Lower Castle Yard, which he had built only a few years earlier, in 1756 (Plate 5). This was handed over to the Ordnance. Eyre claimed to have paid £900 of the £1,612 construction cost himself.[24]

A notice in the Dublin press on 24 April 1762, which announced the reconstitution of the Barrack Board as a board of works, referred to the appointment of three officers to it: Magill as comptroller (as well as being a commissioner), Henry Mitchell as treasurer, and Henry Keene as architect.[25] Keene was described as 'a gentleman of the greatest ability in that science'. Six days later a report was submitted to the Board on the project for which Keene had been specifically brought to Ireland – and which has hitherto been unattributed to him – the complete rebuilding of Palatine Square at the Royal Barracks in Dublin. The document was co-authored by Magill and Keene. This project had originated with a condition report from the Barrack Board, compiled in December 1759 and presented to the Lord Lieutenant, the Duke of Bedford, on 11 January 1760: 'We have also viewed the buildings of the Palatine Square, on which no late repair has been made; and are of the opinion that the front walls [presumably those facing the quadrangle] of that entire building are in so ruinous a state, that they must necessarily be rebuilt.'[26] Eyre had intended to carry out remedial works on the three ranges of the square, to follow modernisation work carried out on the other two principal squares, Horse Square and Royal Square in 1758-59 (Plate 4).[27]

However, a number of alleged defects had been identified in the Barrack Board's report, including the provision of inadequately sized roof timbers in Horse Square and problems with wall loading in the centre block of Royal Square. The Board had asked three independent contractors, described as 'experienced master builders', to carry out an assessment. They were critical of some building elements.

4 – Thomas Burgh, centre block of Horse Square (begun 1703), Royal (Collins) Barracks, Dublin

The original walling material – calp limestone rubble with limestone quoins – is clearly visible, as are the granite window dressings introduced in Thomas Eyre's reconstruction of 1758-59.

5 – Thomas Eyre, Surveyor General's house and office, Lower Castle Yard, Dublin Castle (1756)

Detail of the entrance archway, with coat of arms of the Royal Irish Artillery. Eyre lost the house to the Ordnance Department in 1762, and the arms were presumably affixed at a subsequent date. The Royal Irish Artillery was founded in 1755, and survived as an independent unit until 1801.
(photo Mariga Guinness (before demolition in the 1960s); courtesy Irish Architectural Archive (IAA))

In Royal Square the front wall had an outward deflection above the top of the arcade. The two contractors who signed their reports (dated 21 December 1759), George Stewart and Robert Mack, concluded that the lean was an old one, rather than the result of a recent increase in the superincumbent load on the wall. However, they added that 'the burthen [is now] too great to be trusted on walls in that condition'. This new load was accounted for by the provision of a new cornice, granite reveals and flagged floors in the galleries over the arcade. The third contractor declined to sign on the grounds, it was stated, that he was not familiar with the construction of stonework.[28] Indeed, as the other two had to swear their evidence (before Lyons, Whitelock and Magill), one can see how he was cautious. As Eyre's work had not caused the deflection, it would seem that this was all an irrelevance. However, the covering report of the Barrack Board, signed by all but one of its members (Sandford), claimed that the walls 'from their present warped state, are probably insufficient to bear the great additional weight laid on them in the late repair'. In other words, the building was at risk of collapse. There were further inconsistencies. While the contractors considered the (new) sashes and glazing to be 'good of the kind', the covering report said that the exact opposite. The report said that there was insufficient bond in the wall, but as no new materials had been introduced into the wall proper (the cornice sat on top of it), there was nothing to bond.

Reading between the lines, it appears that the inquiry was stage-managed by Magill in order to undermine public confidence in Eyre's abilities, though the Surveyor General was not named personally. Magill had been down this road before and had played his part in Nevill's downfall, voting for his expulsion from the Commons in 1753. Eyre, however, was determined to expose the whole exercise as a charade, and, unusually for a public servant, was prepared to go into print to do so.

His rebuttal, published very quickly, ran to sixteen octavo pages, considerably longer than the original report, which he answered section by section.[29] The technical details, which are well argued, need not detain us here. While the Barrack Board had consulted three tradesmen, Eyre arranged for no fewer than thirteen (bricklayers, stonecutters and carpenters) to look over the buildings on his behalf. Each group pronounced them sound. All signed their names. Eyre denounced Stewart and Mack, the two supposed 'most experienced master builders', as charlatans whom he had declined to employ. Stewart, he alleged, was a 'mere carpenter' who, while working under Dobbs, had been 'discharged for fraudulent practice'. Mack, 'an obscure journeyman stonecutter', had been dismissed by 'His Majesty's Works in Scotland for misbehaviour'. He claimed each had contradicted the other in their findings (though this is not clear from the report which was jointly signed). He identifies the contractor who declined to sign the report as John Sproule, but says he did so out of a sense of injustice rather than for the reasons stated. Eyre also attacked the Board directly, accusing them of misrepresentation, unfair process and ignorance: 'Most of the Gentlemen who signed the Report of the Commissioners gave little or no attendance at the time that the said survey or inspection were made.' The most serious misrepresentation, in Eyre's view, was the use of the word 'present' to describe the warped state of the wall, implying that the warp was recent, while the 'master builders' had said it was an old settlement. He concluded that if a genuine independent report were to find any defects in the Dublin Barracks, he and the tradesmen responsible would ensure that they were made good without charge to the public purse.

Notwithstanding his published remarks, Eyre proceeded to work on as before, and on 23 April 1760 proposed a four-month building programme for remedial works to Palatine Square.[30] Unsurprisingly, this did not get the go-ahead. A week earlier, the Lord Lieutenant, the Duke of Bedford, had returned to England, leaving Ireland in the charge of the lords justices. The whole episode had been played out in the concluding months of his stay in Dublin. Significantly, Bedford did not have him sacked, and as Parliament could not remove him he was effectively safe until the next lord lieutenant was due in the autumn of 1761. Eyre had served Bedford well, doubling the size of his private apartments at Dublin Castle while he was in England in 1758-59 (Plate 6).[31] A volume of drawings of Irish fortifications, prepared by Eyre in 1754-55, had found a place in Bedford's private library at Woburn.[32] In early 1761, perhaps in an attempt to safeguard his position, Eyre bought himself a seat in Parliament. The breakdown in the relationship between Eyre and the barrack commissioners may well have precipitated Kildare's removal of the Ordnance buildings from their remit at this time. Eyre now busied himself erecting a tower (to be named in honour of Bedford) atop the centre block in the Upper Yard of Dublin Castle, built between 1750 and 1754. Originally conceived as part of Nevill's design for the building, the tower was completed in time for Halifax's arrival, the last fitment – the clock – being inaugurated on the day he was sworn in, 6 October 1761 (Plate 7). The tower and clock thus represented both the pinnacle and the conclusion of Eyre's career as Surveyor General. His time had indeed run out.

In his new architect Keene, Magill had a kindred spirit, for Keene's father too had been a carpenter [33] (while Eyre's had been a landed member of Parliament). In April 1762, Magill and Keene drew up a joint report, reviewing the situation at the Royal Barracks. They claimed that Palatine Square was 'originally an insufficient building [sic] ... incapable of effectual repair' and recommended a rebuild.[34] This was largely a reiteration of the opinion given by the Barrack Board in February 1760. It seems likely that the report had been penned personally by Magill, and what we had now was the added professional endorsement of Keene.

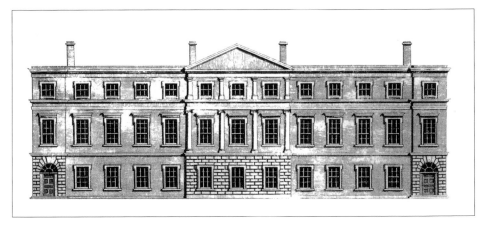

6 – Thomas Eyre, State Apartments, Dublin Castle: elevation to the garden (1758-59)

Engraving by John Lodge, 1779, from a drawing by Robert Pool and John Cash, in their VIEWS OF THE MOST
REMARKABLE PUBLIC BUILDINGS, MONUMENTS AND OTHER EDIFICES IN THE CITY OF DUBLIN (1780). The left-hand doorway
was never built, as a slightly earlier (1753) octagonal tower by Eyre stood in front of the new façade at this point.
An original drawing for this elevation, signed by Eyre's deputy Joseph Jarratt, survives in the Irish Architectural
Archive. The garden front was replaced by a replica in 1964-68.

7 – Joseph Tudor, A PROSPECT OF THE UPPER CASTLE COURT, FROM THE COUNCIL CHAMBER,
DUBLIN, 1753, engraved by Parr

The construction of the Bedford Tower (seen on the right) was not completed by Thomas Eyre until 1761.
The building it crowns was begun by Arthur Jones Nevill in 1750. Tudor, who was employed as a scene painter at the
Castle, clearly had access to the project drawings.

8 – Henry Keene, Palatine Square, Royal Barracks, Dublin (1766-71)

West elevation of the east range, with carriage entrance. The coursed granite walling is very different from Burgh's calp rubble in Horse Square (see Plate 4).

However, the project remained stalled for three years, during most of which Keene probably remained in England. It was only after his former clerk, Euclid Alfray, returned to his service in 1765 that progress was made.[35] In February 1766 the Barrack Board recorded its frustration with Keene, with whom it had difficulty in getting over to attend meetings, such consultations being considered vital for the preparation of comprehensive reports on all the barracks. After a lot of effort he came for one day in December 1765, and disappeared again. Matters were eventually advanced and, in respect of Palatine Square, an estimate of £32,000 was made and a cost benefit analysis carried out.[36] In addition to the rebuilding, the quadrangle was to be closed by a new, fourth range to the east (Plate 8). Tenders were invited in August 1766.[37] Alfray remained in Dublin into 1767, and presumably handed over the project to Keene's successor, Christopher Myers.[38] The project was complete by 1771.[39] The detailing of the granite ashlar facing of the internal elevations and most of the east block (a contrast to the calp limestone elevations of Burgh's buildings) owes much to Keene's earlier work at Trinity College, Dublin, specifically the plain south elevation of the south wing of Parliament Square, facing the Provost's garden (Plates 9, 10). The ground floor of the river front of Palatine Square is faced with limestone blocks and voussoirs and granite dressings, very similar to those of the north elevation at Trinity, facing College Street (Plates 11, 12).[40]

9 – Henry Keene, Palatine Square, Royal Barracks, Dublin (1766-71)

Rebuilt west range, east elevation, detail. The arcade is constructed of granite like the walling above it. While the arcade resembles Burgh's earlier arcade in plan-form, it is unclear what materials he used.

10 – Theodore Jacobsen, Henry Keene and John Sanderson, West Front of Trinity College, Dublin (1752-59)

Detail of the coursed granite walling and parapet of the south elevation of the southern return wing. Compare with the walling in Plate 9.

11 – Palatine Square, Royal Barracks, Dublin (1766-71)

Detail of the squared limestone walling of the south elevation of the south wing (facing the Small Square and the River Liffey). The upper floors of this elevation were constructed from much rougher calp rubble which remained visible until plastered over c.1989. This façade was presumably faced with limestone to tie in with the earlier Burgh buildings facing the river.

12 – West Front of Trinity College, Dublin (1752-59)

Limestone detail of the north elevation of the northern return wing. Compare the walling and voussoirs with those at the barracks in Plate 11.

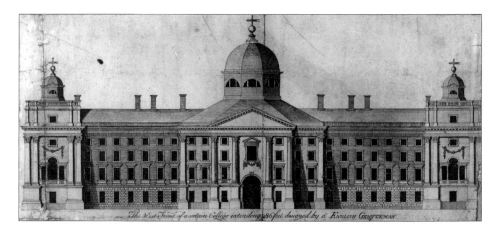

*13 – Theodore Jacobsen, Henry Keene and John Sanderson, new West Front of Trinity College,
Dublin, as proposed in 1757*

*Engraved from a drawing by John Aheron, architect. The north pavilion had been modified in execution after 1752.
It also had the only one of the three domes to be completed, though it was subsequently taken down.
(courtesy Trinity College, Dublin)*

Of great interest is the fact that Magill had received an honorary doctorate of laws from the college in the spring of 1760.[41] In seeking an explanation for this singular honour, normally reserved for aristocrats or for the holders of high office, we may find the background to the whole Eyre/Keene debacle.

The rebuilding of the West Front of Trinity College in the 1750s was effectively a public works project, since it was entirely paid for by Parliament and, indeed, was referred to in contemporary account books as Parliament Buildings (Plate 13). The square around which they were ranged was known as Parliament Square. The development was to be the architectural swansong of the octogenarian Richard Baldwin, Provost since 1717. The three ranges which were built consisted of relatively plain north and south wings and a west wing (the West Front proper), with an ornate façade and end pavilions. There was to have been a fourth side, adjoining Richard Castle's campanile, but this was never built.[42] The West Front proper replaced an ornate classical range dating from the seventeenth century (Plate 14). However, while the old building had been begun with a bequest left by Sir Hierome Alexander in 1670,[43] by the 1750s the college was pleading poverty and seeking public funds for its replacement. In this they were spectacularly successful, obtaining a total of £45,000 between 1751 and 1757.[44] As this money, though nominally granted by the king, came from revenue surpluses which the Irish parliament would otherwise lose to Britain, the arrangement suited everybody.[45]

The overseer of the project was to be Hugh Darley (a stonecutter and architect), appointed by the college board on 13 July 1752, who was to 'examine all

14 – Old West Front (Sir Hierome Alexander's Building),
Trinity College, Dublin

Engraving from Charles Brooking's Map of Dublin (1728). The northern half of the façade was built in the 1670s
from the designs of Thomas Lucas. The remainder, including the centrepiece, was constructed between 1684 and
1699, apparently under the superintendence of Sir William Robinson.

bills'.[46] As noted, the new buildings were designed by the London amateur Theodore Jacobsen, while the plans and elevations were prepared by Keene and John Sanderson (who were paid £74 by Parliament).[47] However, it seems that the familiar figure of John Magill also played a part. The name 'Mr Magill' is inscribed on the cover of an early folio of project accounts (for 1752-53) in the college muniments.[48] If Magill was checking the accounts, was it for the college or for Parliament? The latter seems more likely since the college had plenty of expertise without him; in addition to Darley as overseer (project manager), both Richard King and William Purfield were employed as measurers.

More significantly, we should ask what happened in February 1755 to cause a rethink in the design of the West Front, prompted by the representations of an unidentified 'gentleman'. The college board delegated Darley to seek the advice of Jacobsen as the original designer. A letter was sent through one John Keene asking what alterations might receive Jacobsen's 'consent and approbation'. An urgent reply was sought to avoid holding up the works. The 'gentleman', Darley wrote, 'has lately taken a tour of Europe and is allowed to have made very judicious observations in the Architectonic way.'[49] What he desired was no less that the deletion of the proposed domes from the centrepiece and end pavilions, on the basis that such features are 'no where to be met in Italy in such buildings', and the narrowing of the breakfront by two bays. Darley concluded: 'All these particulars I must beg you will answer in the most explicit manner in your power for you know that we Irish are somewhat thick headed...'

At this time the north range was largely complete and its pavilion had been erected to just below cornice level. Changes to the design had already being carried out in a most unorthodox way – by demolition. As Darley's letter was been written, a newly erected engaged temple front in the centre of the north range was being taken down. Much of the cut-stone work to the pavilion too had been lately dismantled for a new window arrangement.[50] As Darley's letter indicates, the college board was divided on at least some of the additional changes. However, the opinions of the 'gentleman' did not take effect until after much further unproductive work was done. Thus, the dome and vane on the north pavilion were allowed to proceed, but were ultimately dismantled in November 1757. The breakfront, only begun after the old Robinson centrepiece was demolished in April 1755, was not narrowed, but the substructure for the central dome was constructed, with a vast brick octagon rising through the upper floor levels, before being cut down in late 1758.[51] It may thus be implied that instructions were given by the board in 1757 to eliminate the subsidiary pavilion domes only. Whoever the gentleman was, he clearly had the support of some members of the college board, and they in turn must have been happy that the changes and reconstructions would not be hampered by parliamentary scrutiny. The college was obliged to go to it periodically for each tranche of funding. By early 1755 only £15,000 had been voted towards the project; a further £20,000 would be sought by the end of the year. While it would be tempting to blame (or credit) Magill for the redesign, there is no evidence that he took a tour of Europe. Yet he was involved. An examination of the building accounts reveals that Magill had supplied and been paid for all the sheet lead (a total of sixteen tons) for the north range, corner pavilion and dome.[52] This had been imported by him from Wales, and delivered to the site for fixing by the plumbing contractor William Murphy. Just two tons of lead were needed for the pavilion dome. However, one can calculate from the only known depiction of the domed elevation[53] that at least 136 tons of lead would have been needed for the centre dome. The omission of the domes would therefore constitute a major loss of profit to the supplier. It seems unlikely that Magill's aesthetic sense would have overruled his pocket.

A more likely suspect is Francis Andrews (1718-1774), Trinity's rising star. While he was not appointed to the college board until 1753, it has been suggested that his influence as a senior fellow 'was probably important in obtaining from parliament the grants for the rebuilding of Front [Parliament] Square'.[54] A native of Derry, he was a practising lawyer, aspiring politician, half-hearted academic, and ardent Italophile. However, there is only anecdotal evidence that Andrews had visited Italy at this time, his well-documented grand tour took place in 1766-67.[55] If the 'gentleman' did indeed exist, he clearly carried some weight, even though Darley allowed in his letter that Jacobsen might reasonably refuse to change the design. It seems probable that he did refuse, as perhaps he was meant to. However, the progressive element in the college board clearly revisited the issue more than two years later, and prevailed in having the changes made. Back in 1755 the conservative element would have weighed up another factor besides the aesthetic one – how to placate Magill. The progressives must have subsequently come to some arrangement with him. That Andrews was at the head of this faction may be implied by the fact that within weeks of his installation as Provost on 28 October 1758 (a month after Baldwin's death) the brick octagon had been demolished. According to one source, by this time Andrews and Magill were friends (Plate 15).

It is worth noting that the funds drawn down by the college greatly exceeded the actual cost of building the three ranges of the West Front. By late 1758, when the project was virtually complete, just under £28,000 had been expended but over £43,000 had been transferred from the exchequer to the college account. Andrews had his eye on the surplus: far removed from the archetypal clergyman provost, he was planning to build himself an elegant new house, after a design by Palladio, on the corner of Grafton Street (Plate 16). He had also successfully lobbied for a large increase in salary. Like his predecessor, Provost Baldwin, he paid obeisance to the Whigs. He had befriended both the Lord Lieutenant, the Duke of Bedford, and the Chief Secretary, Richard Rigby, to whom the college awarded a timely honorary doctorate in 1758.

As the imbalance in the accounts must have been evident long before 1758, one suspects that Magill had been brought on board at an early stage and that he helped ensure that the college kept the surplus after the figures were disclosed to Parliament in 1759. This enabled Andrews to proceed with the house, plans being

15 – Theodore Jacobsen, Henry Keene and John Sanderson,
West Front of Trinity College, Dublin (1752-59)

Mid-19th-century photograph showing the West Front as completed in 1759 (courtesy Chandler Collection, IAA)

16 – John Smyth (possibly in collaboration with Henry Keene), Provost's House,
Trinity College, Dublin (begun 1759)

Detail of first-floor façade. Built for Provost Francis Andrews. The ground floor was extended with the doubling in
size of the north pavilion by Provost Hely Hutchinson in 1775 under the superintendence of Christopher Myers.

obtained by June of that year.[56] No separate accounts were published for it, or even isolated in the building records, the whole being thrown in with the costs for the West Front. According to another Trinity fellow, Dr Patrick Duigenan, writing in 1777, the house cost £11,000 to erect.[57] Given the extent to which the college board had indulged itself in its building projects, without any recourse to its estates or investments, an honorary doctorate for Magill must have seemed cheap at the price. Whether the Provost and fellows considered him to be their intellectual equal – the man whose noble acquiescence had saved them from architectural solecism – or simply as someone to be bought off, is another matter. Perhaps significantly, the award of the degree is not recorded in the usual place in the college register. One suspects that Andrews did not have the full support of his board on this occasion. The timing too is interesting since it seems that only the external shell of the Provost's House had been designed by early 1760, when the degree was awarded. It may be that Andrews, with the money in the bank, wanted a free hand with the (sumptuous) interior, and that the honorary degree was a message that no further assistance was needed, thank you. Whatever the case, events were about to unfold which would terminate the friendship between the two men.

The catalyst for this was not the publication of the Barrack Board report, nor indeed Eyre's response, but the death in March 1760 of the Dublin-born actress Peg Woffington (Plate 17). Woffington had many talents and a flock of male followers. She also left a volume of memoirs, published within a short time of her demise. The mention therein of a thinly disguised 'Frank Anderson' prompted the author of *Butter-milk Jack* into print, for Magill too, he alleged, had been one of her admirers, having known her since her youth, both being employed by the impresaria Madame Violante (Woffington as a child star, Magill as a comic turn). The overall tone of the biography is of a man who rose from poor but honest origins, to government employment and a seat in parliament through unscrupulous means. There are allegations of sharp business practice in paying contractors and preparing accounts, but little of a specific nature apart from a reference to a court case, which seems to have followed the Eyre affair. (Magill lost the action.) One gets the impression that the author is playing a balancing act, that his anonymity is dependant on not giving too much away. Much of the text is ridiculous, but as befits successful satire, there is a ring of truth in it, even in the allegations of degeneracy.

It seems clear that while the general purpose in writing 'the adventures of

17 – John Lewis (fl.1737-69), Peg Woffington, oil on canvas

Woffington (c.1718-60), the daughter of a Dublin bricklayer, was a child star with Madame Violante's company in the city before making her name on the London stage. Her admirers included John Magill MP, first comptroller of the works at the Barrack Board, and Francis Andrews, the Provost of Trinity College.
(courtesy Royal Dublin Society)

Buttermilk Jack', as Magill was tagged, was to damage his public standing, there was another, more focused agenda. This was not to help Eyre, whose plight is not mentioned, but to undermine the relationship between Andrews and Magill. The biography alludes to a specific incident of which the writer purported to have inside knowledge. This concerned an evening on which Andrews asked Magill to accompany him on a social call to Woffington's lodgings. Andrews allegedly made a fuss of thanking Woffington for having secured the provostship for him. Her stony silence, however, nonplussed him, and, somewhat embarrassed, he stepped backwards only to fall over a chair. With a bleeding head wound he made his excuses and left. Magill stayed on, made an impression, and spent the night in madame's bed. In a quickly issued second edition of *Butter-milk Jack*, the author gleefully reported that Magill had accused Andrews of having written the pamphlet and had terminated their friendship. The accomplished style and the many literary quotations and epigrams in *Butter-milk Jack* does suggest a well-educated author, but it is hard to see how Andrews might have benefited from its publication. Perhaps there was an honest man in Trinity, outraged at the Provost's money-grubbing antics. The honorary degree may have been a step too far, and perhaps, for Magill, something best forgotten.

As for Andrews, he completed his palace where he lived the life of a wealthy bachelor (provosts had to be unmarried), attended by two of his relatives, a Mr and Mrs Gamble, and a retinue of servants.[58] In 1768 he presided over the installation of his old friend, the Duke of Bedford, as Vice Chancellor of the university. Yet his critics still breathed, and in 1772 one of them felt compelled to resurrect the old scandal in an anonymous tract, alleging that 'it was well known [that Andrews had] lived in the closest intimacy with Mrs Woffington ... at this hour the chief ornaments of the Provost's house [are] the portraits of that celebrated courtezan in various characters and attitudes.'[59] The author of this 'letter' was reputedly Hercules Langrishe, a patriot politician appointed to the Barrack Board in 1766.

This episode is of interest in our story because its publication coincided with another stroke by Andrews. In June 1772 he successfully lobbied the Lord Lieutenant, the notoriously corrupt Viscount Townshend, to appoint another of his Gamble relatives to the Barrack Board at a salary of £400 a year.[60] This followed the retirement of Magill and three other commissioners. One can see how Langrishe would have resented the foisting of so obvious a placeman on him and his colleagues. Yet, as always with Andrews, there was an attractive woman in the background. Townshend and Andrews were both admirers of the latest young beauty, Dolly Monroe, a niece of Lady Loftus. Langrishe had in some way been involved too, though, seeing as he was married, this may just have been just a family connection. Lady Loftus's husband had been a colleague on the Barrack Board. The college register, that most terse of tomes, contains the surprising transcript of a codicil to Andrews' will leaving instructions for Dolly to receive 'coloured prints (a fitter ornament for her dressing room than my library) as a mark of respect and Regard for her many amiable Qualities'.[61] McParland has suggested that these were the pictures of Woffington, but this seems too crass even for Andrews.[62] For the Provost's supporters, the slight was not that he was one of Peg's admirers – that was admitted (albeit in an aesthetic sense) – but that he should have depended on her influence for his appointment.[63] What Dubliners may have also found particularly humorous were the Provost's poetic musings about her, referred to in *Butter-milk Jack*, and the risqué verses he had allegedly ghost-written for Peg, to present to an earlier viceroy, the Duke of Dorset. Probably not generally known was that not only was Andrews a trustee of Woffington's will, but so also were three other prominent Dublin lawyers, among them Eyre Trench, the first cousin of the Surveyor General, and Edmond Sexton Pery, a future speaker of the Irish Commons.[64] All were members of the Middle Temple. However, Dolly's prints were to be the least of Trinity's worries. It was discovered that Andrews had leased some of the Provost's estates to his Gamble relatives, effectively alienating the properties. While the transactions seem to have been ill-conceived rather than fraudulent, Andrews' successor, Provost Hely Hutchinson, a trained lawyer, determined on court action. This too was ill-conceived. The college ultimately lost and was forced to settle, with huge legal costs.

Whatever the precise nature of Magill's connection with Trinity, he was undoubtedly involved with the college at the time that the West Front was being built from Henry Keene's working drawings. Keene, it will be remembered, was paid for these by the Irish parliament. Therefore, I would suggest, Magill would have been familiar with Keene's abilities long before Halifax's appointment as Lord Lieutenant, and was also in a position to further advance his career in securing a government appointment for him. Indeed, Magill would have been familiar also with the abilities of the carpenter George Stewart (an old contact from the Dobbs era), who, having earned almost £6,000 from the Trinity job, was invited by him to comment on Eyre's work at the Barracks. The fact that Keene would be an absentee would also suit Magill's purposes at the Barrack Board, as it would leave more power and authority in his hands as comptroller of the works. Eyre's challenge to the commissioners' authority had to be met. In persuading Halifax not only to remove him, but to install their own man in his place, they had the perfect solution.

Before we dispose of Magill, mention might be made of the maintenance arrangements for the largest Dublin public building not under the control of the Board of Works. That was the Royal Hospital Kilmainham, which had its own architect, or 'overseer', paid by the governors. In the early years, the post used to go to the Surveyor General anyway, Robinson being followed by Burgh, Pearce, Dobbs

18 – Anon., Deputy Master's House, Royal Hospital, Kilmainham (1762/63)

*The hospital governors appointed John Magill, 'a proper person of integrity and experience in architecture'
to superintend the erection of the house, designed by another, unknown, hand. The contractors included Magill's old
friend, the carpenter George Stewart. The house, constructed on the site of a seventeenth-century flanker, was
originally L-shaped; the two bays to the right were added from the designs of Sir John Trail in 1797.*

and Nevill. However, Nevill was retained by the hospital for some years after he lost office as Surveyor General in 1752, despite rather aggressive petitions by Eyre in 1756 and 1758. After the second petition, they decided to do without an architect altogether,[65] and it was not until April 1762 that the matter was reviewed. In a clear statement that Eyre was out of favour and that there was a new power in the land, the hospital governors entrusted the execution of their new Deputy Master's House to Magill – 'a proper person of integrity and experience in architecture' – even though plans had apparently been drawn up by another hand, an architect who is mysteriously not named in the minute books (Plate 18).[66]

To return to the administrative chronology, Eyre continued to work as Chief Engineer of the Ordnance until the spring of 1766, when a new patent was granted to Henry Mark Mason. He continued to sit in Parliament up until the time of his death in 1772, actually expiring in the chamber.[67] Magill left Parliament in 1768 and the Barrack Board in 1772.

The various arrangements under which the Barrack Board operated were formalised by the Civil List Act passed in the Irish parliament in 1793 (33 Geo. III c.34, I.), which decreed that all public buildings erected solely at the public expense were to be placed under the control of 'his majesty's board of works'.[68] It was probably from this period that the Barrack Board became known collectively as the Barrack Board and Board of Works. It was one board, the Board of Works being a sub-committee. The Act was presented to the (Irish) House of Commons on 18 June 1793 as a 'Bill for the better regulation of that branch of the public expenditure, which relates to the erection and repair of Public Buildings'.[69] The Act is important in providing the legislation under which the Irish Board of Works, in its various guises, was to erect buildings for the duration of the period under study. Section XXI of the Act was as follows:

> And be it enacted and declared, that all public buildings or works or any kind whatsoever, carried out solely at the public expence [sic], shall be hereafter in the execution of the same, under the sole management, inspection, and controul [sic] of his majesty's board of works and to provide for the due and faithful execution of the work, the lord lieutenant as soon as conveniently may be after the passing of this act, shall appoint by warrant, an architect or inspector of civil buildings, (he being bona fide an architect or builder), who shall superintend the execution of all public works, under the direction of the commissioners of the board of works, and who is hereby declared, and shall be incapable of sitting or voting in parliament.

Two further sections of the Act, XXII and XXIII, are also important. Under section XXII, works ordered by the Lord Lieutenant with an estimated value under £100 could be contracted for by the 'commissioners of the board of works' without further consultation. Works with a higher value required the Lord Lieutenant's approval prior to the placing of a contract. Section XXIII refers to inspections of the works, the issuing of architect's certificates, and payment thereon.

From 1762 the Barrack Board had two effective architectural posts on the establishment. One, the 'architect to the Board', was apparently the senior official, chiefly responsible for barracks; the other held the title of 'clerk and inspector of civil buildings in Dublin', amended to 'architect and inspector...' in 1788.[70] Henry Keene, first holder of the architect post, was succeeded by Christopher Myers (c.1725-1789) from 1767 to 1776, by Christopher and Graham Myers from 1777 to 1783, and by William Gibson from 1784 to 1793. Graham Myers, who had moved to the barrack inspectorate, returned to the post of architect in 1793, holding it until 1801 (jointly with John Gibson from 1799). The first clerk and inspector was Joseph Jarratt, from 1763 to 1774. His appointment ensured continuity on the civil side as he had previously served as Eyre's deputy (from 1753). Jarratt was followed by Thomas Cooley (1740-1784), from 1775 to 1784, and by Thomas Penrose (1740-1792), from 1785 to 1792.[71] It was during Penrose's term of office that rank of clerk was amended to architect. Vincent Waldré (c.1742-1814), who was appointed on Penrose's death in 1792, continued in office under the terms of the 1793 Act. Italian by birth, Waldré (originally called Valdrati) was a protégé of the Lord Lieutenant, the Marquess of Buckingham, who had brought him to Ireland in 1787.[72] The sequence of architects at the Royal Hospital Kilmainham only partly overlaps with the appointments of architects and inspectors of civil buildings. Cooley advised the hospital from 1774 up until his death ten years later, but he was followed by Robert Parke rather than by Penrose. Parke was, in turn, succeeded by Sir John Trail, architect of the nearby Kilmainham Gaol, who died in 1801.

It is noticeable that while the Board of Works had never been, and, indeed, would never be a branch of its English equivalent, three of the above architects were English-born: Keene, Myers and Cooley. This was a period in which prominent English architects began to be employed by private clients also, though it should be noted that both Myers and Cooley had settled in Ireland before their official appointments. Myers, originally a joiner from Whitehaven in Cumbria, was employed by the Earl of Antrim at Glenarm from 1754, but later moved to Dublin. According to one source, his Barrack Board appointment in 1767 was due to the influence of John Hely Hutchinson MP.[73] After Hely Hutchinson became Provost of Trinity College in 1774, he appointed him college architect at £150 a year (four times the pay of a junior fellow), even though the only work allegedly carried out by him in his first two years was to extend the Provost's House at a cost of £300.[74] Cooley, as is well known, arrived in Dublin to carry out his competition-winning design of 1768 for the Royal Exchange (now City Hall). Symptomatic of the turn to London for big names was the proposal in 1773 by the (Irish) Revenue Commissioners for a new Dublin custom house on the downstream side of the Anglesea Street/Moore Street axis. With their petition to the Lord Lieutenant, they enclosed draft layout plans by Myers, but proposed that 'Sir William Chambers or some other eminent architect' should be approached for a definitive design for an 'elegant but simple building'.[75] In the event, it was Chambers' pupil James Gandon whom they employed, and who arrived in Dublin in early 1781.

In 1775 Chambers was brought in to finish Parliament Square in Trinity College, though initially by erecting a theatre (examination hall) and a chapel to terminate the south and north ranges, rather than by constructing a fourth, east, range. A fourth range was designed but was never built (Plate 19).[76] Myers was to justify his retainer by superintending the erection of the theatre (begun 1777), while the chapel (begun after 1787) was carried out by his son Graham.

By the end of 1794, the awkwardly titled Barrack Board and Board of Works was complaining that its workload had been greatly increased by the 1793 legislation. It would appear that it was the regulations drawn up under the Act which pro-

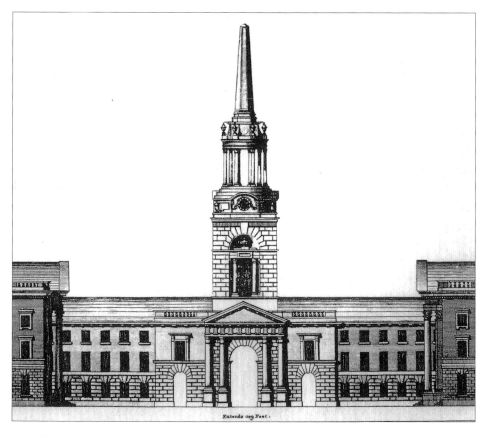

19 – Sir William Chambers, intended chapel and public theatre, Trinity College, Dublin

Drawn by Robert Pool and John Cash, and engraved by John Lodge, for their VIEWS OF DUBLIN (1780).
The central block, with its Doric temple front, is derived from the base of the then existing bell tower of Richard
Castle. While Chambers' design remained unexecuted, Castle's tower was taken down in the 1790s.

vided for the Board of Works component to function as a sub-committee, consisting of three members of the full nine-member Barrack Board and Board of Works. The three members comprised a first commissioner (paid a salary of £200) and two other commissioners (each paid £100). The complaints were outlined in two memorials which were sent to the Lord Lieutenant on 11 December 1794. One was a petition from five members of the Barrack Board and Board of Works; the other, a covering letter with some dissenting comments, was from one of the petitioners, James Cuffe (1748-1821).[77]

Cuffe, a member of the Barrack Board and Board of Works since 1772, had been created Superintendent General of Barracks in 1776. The three-member Board of Works had complained that since a quorum of three was required, they were unable to perform their other Barrack Board duties, or indeed to leave the office. The memorial asked for a total of five Barrack Board members to be appointed to the Board of Works so that the 'business of both Departments might be carried on with due attention and advantage...' It is not clear if their request was granted before a further, major change occurred in 1799.

Cuffe, who was also MP for county Mayo (since 1768) and a rising political star, was promoted to head the Barrack Board in 1796 at a salary of £600. He was elevated to the peerage as Baron Tyrawley in 1797. Since 1777 it had been the practice for the Commander in Chief (of the army in Ireland) to sit as an unpaid member of the Board.[78] After the outbreak of insurrection in Ireland in May 1798, the Marquess Cornwallis was appointed both Lord Lieutenant and Commander in Chief, effectively a military governor. Cornwallis, who had been Master General of the (British) Ordnance since 1795, took a seat on the Barrack Board, where Tyrawley was the senior permanent member. After the suppression of the insurrection, Cornwallis undertook a number of political changes, one of which, in 1799, was to appoint Tyrawley to take direct charge of the barracks. This was effected by an Act of Parliament (39 Geo. III c.26, I.), passed on 7 May 1799, which was supposed to solve the problem of travel, complained of in 1794. From July 1799 the Commander in Chief and another ex officio member, the Quartermaster General, ceased to sit on the Board. The Act was purportedly based on a section of the letters patent of 1759, though this assertion was to be challenged almost twenty years later.[79] While the Act indicated that the vesting of powers in a single commissioner (or commissioners) appointed by the Lord Lieutenant might be a temporary expediency, Tyrawley's authority became a permanent arrangement. It would appear that from this date the Barrack Board ceased to have anything to do with barracks, though its title remained Barrack Board and Board of Works. Under section III of the Act, all the commissioners were to exercise powers as a Board of Works, but with respect to civil buildings only.[80] Tyrawley functioned as both Commissioner for Barracks and as chairman of the board, on which he sat when his presence was required for a quorum. This solved the problem of inspecting buildings around the country. That function was now reserved for Tyrawley as barrack commissioner. The other commissioners had no need to travel since all the civil buildings were located in Dublin. This concentrated power put Tyrawley in a stronger position than any public works officer since the abolition of the post of Surveyor General of Fortifications and Buildings almost forty years earlier. The *Gentleman's and Citizen's Almanack* for 1800 shows the Barrack Board and Board of Works divided into two branches, military and civil, sharing an office in Merrion Street. However, only under the civil branch is a board of commissioners listed, with Tyrawley at its head. The commander in chief had ceased to be a member of the Board.[81] In the military branch, Tyrawley is listed as Barrack Master General, with Lieutenant Colonel Quin John Freeman as his deputy.

EARLY NINETEENTH CENTURY

On 1 January 1801 the Act of Union came into effect, the final chapter of Cornwallis's political reorganisation. With the uniting of the parliaments of Britain and Ireland, changes were made in the organisation of the military establishment. The Irish Board of Ordnance was abolished. The duties of the Chief Engineer, or director, of the Ordnance Department were now to be taken over by the commanding Royal Engineer for Ireland, appointed by the British Board of Ordnance.[82] The Barrack Board and Board of Works, however, remained independent of the Royal Engineers. On 25 May 1801, Philip Yorke, Earl of Hardwicke, landed, and was sworn in as Lord Lieutenant. Hardwicke (assisted by his Chief Secretary Henry Abbott) determined to proceed beyond Cornwallis's reforms, and decreed, on 31 December, that the military and civil divisions were to be formally separated. The Military Branch became the Barrack Department, under Tyrawley and still with no board. Tyrawley held the title of Chief Commissioner of Barracks and Deputy Barrack Master General. The Civil Branch was to be known as the Board of Works, a civil body which was sometimes referred to as the Civil Buildings Commissioners. No new patent was issued, the Commissioners somewhat confusingly retaining their old patent as the Barrack Board and Board of Works. While the existing board members were retained, there was a reorganisation of staff. The first meeting of the new civil board took place, with Tyrawley in the chair, on 12 January 1802. Immediately, they requested separate accommodation, away from the Barrack Department.[83] However, new premises were not obtained until 1806.[84]

Hardwicke drew up regulations (based on the 1793 Act) for the operation of the new civil board. Among these regulations was the stipulation (taken from the Act) that any estimate over £100 required the Lord Lieutenant's written authority before works could be contracted for.[85] Hardwicke immediately removed from office the Architect and Inspector of Civil Buildings, Vincent Waldré, transferring him to the barrack inspectorate. Waldré did, however, retain the independent post of architect to the Royal Hospital, which he had held since the death of Trail in the previous year. In place of Waldré at the Board of Works, Hardwicke appointed Robert Woodgate, who had originally come to Ireland as carpenter (*plus ça change*) to Sir John Soane. Woodgate and the measurer John Behan were sworn into office at the 12 January meeting.

From the start there were irregularities. There was friction between the two

20 – *Thomas Clement Thompson RHA, Francis Johnston (1823)*

Drawing, engraved by Henry Meyer, and inscribed 'member of the Royal Hibernian Academy and Architect of the Board of Works Ireland'. Johnston was Architect and Inspector of Civil Buildings from 1805 to 1826. In the background is his General Post Office, Dublin (1814-18) (courtesy IAA)

opposite, top

21 – *Francis Johnston, Chapel Royal, Dublin Castle (1807-14)*

Interior, photographed c.1898. The chapel was sumptuously decorated with decorative plasterwork by George Stapleton, incorporating heads modelled by Edward and John Smyth, and wood carvings (including the capitals and gallery fronts) by Richard Stewart. The viceroy's pew, with its bow front, is in the left-hand gallery. (courtesy IAA)

officers, Woodgate attempting within months to have Behan dismissed.[86] Woodgate paid little attention to the regulations, obtaining retrospective sanction directly from the Lord Lieutenant to pay the contractors employed in enlarging the Vice-Regal Lodge.[87] The architectural genius of the age, James Gandon, who, as has been stated, was never an officer of the Board of Works, also fell foul of the new regime. In late 1801 he had been asked by the Chief Secretary to produce plans for a new Chapel Royal at Dublin Castle, but was reluctant to cut across Waldré. Being reassured that new arrangements were about to be made with regard to the Board of Works (Waldré was to be replaced), he produced seven different designs, some after Woodgate's appointment. However, despite obtaining approval, he withdrew from the project, professing himself 'ready to explain many particulars to Mr Woodgate [the jumped-up carpenter] for better understanding of my Ideas in Order to make my Design more perfect, presuming that in some future establishment I may not be undeserving of notice'.[88] The lack of accountability may have stemmed in part from the refusal of General Freeman (who in 1803 succeeded Tyrawley both as Chief

right

22 – W. Flavelle, south view of the Record Tower, Dublin Castle, engraved by James Basire, 1813

This view, printed to accompany a report on the Public Records of Ireland, shows the following works by Francis Johnston: the Chapel Royal; the two-storey State Paper Office; and the reconstructed thirteenth-century Wardrobe or Record Tower. To the left is one bay of Thomas Eyre's garden front to the State Apartments (1758-59) (see also plate 6), linked at second-floor level by the private corridor to the Viceroy's pew in the chapel. (from the Parliamentary Papers, H.C. 1812-13 [351.] xv. 547; courtesy IAA)

Commissioner of Barracks and as chairman of the Board of Works) to involve himself with civil buildings until offered a similar £600 stipend in 1806.

A new patent was issued to the Board of Works (archaically termed the Commissioners and Overseers of Barracks and Public Works in Ireland) on 19 June 1810, the term being at the monarch's pleasure.[89] However, in 1811 it was the Board's turn to come under parliamentary scrutiny as part of an examination into the running of all government departments, begun as far back as 1780.[90] This was published in 1812. Irregularities were found in the Board's operations.[91] It transpired that lords lieutenant ordered work directly from the architect, and that the costs were paid out of supplementary budgets. Woodgate, who had died in 1805, was singled out for attack. His successor, Francis Johnston (1760-1829) (Plates 1, 20), was queried about his inability to erect buildings in accordance with his estimates, specifically the huge cost overrun on the new Chapel Royal at Dublin Castle (from £9,533 to £42,350) since construction had begun in 1807. He successfully argued about increases in the cost of materials and other misfortunes, and emerged from the inquiry unscathed (Plates 21, 22) – this despite such irregularities as the substitution of cut-stone elevations for stucco without approval. The select committee, however, was not impressed by the performance of the Board, whose seven members (paid a total of £3,000 per annum) had little to do but pass Johnston's accounts. It recommended that the Board be abolished, and that in future the works should to be carried out directly by the architect, reporting to the government. The chairman would retain his barrack position. It was suggested, however, that in the event of a future amalgamation of the military and civil departments, a new board of commissioners might be appointed. It should be noted that Johnston's importance was not just that he was Architect and Inspector of Civil Buildings for the Board of Works, but that he advised the Irish government in examining plans for courthouses and gaols all over the country, although they were erected by the Grand Juries.[92] He had also succeeded Waldré as architect to the RHK in late 1804, some months after he first began advising the governors on building matters. Johnston was also architect for the Richmond Asylum in Dublin, begun in 1810 (Plate 23). He was subsequently appointed architect to the Commissioners for the Erection of Lunatic Asylums, established under an Act of 1817 (57 Geo. III c.106).

In 1817 legislation was passed providing for the termination of the Board of Works, among other bodies and sinecures, with provision for the Lord Lieutenant or the Treasury to appoint an officer or officers to undertake 'all duties connected with the superintendence of the public buildings'.[93] This should have paved the way for Johnston (or a successor) to take over the running of the civil department directly, as the select committee had recommended.[94] Johnston might not have been over-enthusiastic about assuming additional administrative duties; by 1821 he was proposing

23 – Francis Johnston, Richmond Asylum, Dublin (1810-15), with corner pavilion by William Murray (1836)

The first of Johnston's asylum designs, it had a hollow square plan, probably based on the layout of Robert Reid's Morningside Asylum, Edinburgh, published in 1807. The front range is seen here in 1995, a year after the demolition of the other three sides.

24 – Francis Johnston, Royal Hibernian Academy, Lower Abbey Street, Dublin (1824)

Johnston not only designed the academy but paid for its construction,. donating £14,000. The building was burnt out during the Easter Rising of 1916; only the upper part of the façade survives. (RIAI Murray Collection, IAA)

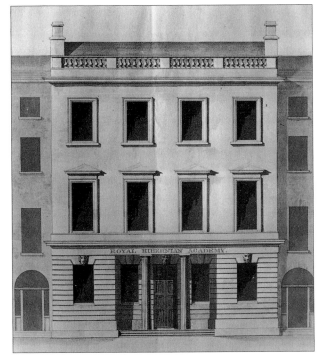

25 – Martin Cregan PRHA
(attrib.), William Murray,
oil on canvas

This is possibly the portrait
exhibited by Cregan at the RHA in
1844. Murray (1789-1849) was
Architect and Inspector of Civil
Buildings from 1822 to 1832,
initially (until 1826) in a joint
capacity with his cousin and
master Francis Johnston.
(collection Royal Hibernian
Academy, on loan to RIAI)

to retire altogether.[95] He was one of the promoters of the new Royal Hibernian
Academy, granted a charter of incorporation in that year. He was eventually to
donate £14,000 to it for the construction of a new building on Abbey Street (Plate
24). In the event, Johnston did not leave the public service, but arranged for his
cousin and long-time assistant, William Murray (1789-1849) (Plate 25), to be
appointed joint Architect and Inspector of Civil Buildings with him in 1822. None
of the commissioners, however, was dismissed, provision being made only for their
posts to be left vacant 'upon the Termination of the present existing Interests'. They
were not in a hurry to go, so a further Act had to be passed in 1824 providing for
their pensions.[96] This Act also had an important amendment stipulating that as each
commissioner retired, his post was to be abolished rather than simply left vacant. As
only a few members availed of this provision the Act had no immediate effect.
However, the Act was significant in that it provided the legal mechanism whereby
the building functions of the old Board were eventually transferred in 1832 to new
Commissioners of Public Works. The relevant Section I of the 1824 Act stated:

after the Offices of the said Commissioners [the old Board of Works] shall become vacant, it shall and may be lawful for the Lord Lieutenant or other Chief Governor or Governors of Ireland for the time being in concurrence with the Lord High Treasurer, or the Commissioners of His Majesty's Treasury for the time being, to make such Arrangement as shall provide for the sufficient Execution of All Duties connected with the Superintendence of the Public Buildings under the charge of the said Board of Works.

It is noteworthy also that the 1824 Act deleted the reference to the appointment of one or more officers, leaving the simple term 'Arrangement as shall provide'.

In the meantime, military buildings continued to be controlled by the Barrack Department. In 1821, however, an Act (1 & 2 Geo. IV c.69) was passed transferring title to buildings in England occupied by the Ordnance Department under the Crown to their board of principal officers. This was followed by a further Act in 1822 (3 Geo. IV c.108) which transferred title to all barracks in Great Britain and Ireland to the Ordnance officers. The consequence of this was that the 'Board of Ordnance ... became the sole authority for the construction and maintenance of barracks in the United Kingdom'.[97] By 1824 the Barrack Department in Ireland had been placed under the control of the 'principal officers of His Majesty's Ordnance';[98] by 1825 it had ceased to be listed as a separate department.[99] To anticipate, the Board of Ordnance continued to be responsible for barracks throughout the kingdom until 1855, when it was abolished and its building functions ceded to the Royal Engineers.

It may seem extraordinary that the (civil) Board of Works, condemned to oblivion in 1812, should survive for almost another twenty years. Whatever about the salaries of the commissioners, politically its operations were seldom contentious. In the context of public works generally in Ireland, the maintenance of public buildings in Dublin gave little employment and was of little interest to politicians. It was the construction of such things as roads, bridges, canals, piers, harbours and railways that exercised the minds of the parliamentary select committee that sat during the late 1820s.[100] In 1830, at the conclusion of these deliberations, the Knight of Kerry, Vice Treasurer for Ireland, recommended to Wellington, the Prime Minister, that new public works legislation should include the following clauses: 'All works for which public money has been advanced ... be vested in a body of commissioners to be appointed by the Treasury for their custody and maintenance, for which are to be excepted all schools, colleges, churches and glebe houses' and 'Also [that] all public buildings, and all expenditure thereon ... be conducted by said commissioners and accounts passed by them.'[101] In the event these duties were added after the enactment of the legislation of 1831.

THE ACT OF 1831

One of the aims of the legislation was to reduce the number and expense of the various boards and commissioners then in operation, the savings on salaries being estimated at £1,300. However because there was a famine in 1831, the greatest urgency in passing the Public Works Act (1 & 2 Wm IV c.33) was to make available the £500,000 voted by Parliament for loans and grants.[102] It was envisaged when the bill was being debated in the House that additional duties would be assigned to the new Commissioners of Public Works after its enactment. On 30 June 1831, the Chief Secretary for Ireland, Rt Hon Edward Stanley, told the house that 'it was intended to do away with the Board of Works' among other boards; on 31 August 1831, Thomas Spring Rice MP, Secretary of the Treasury, stated that the new Commissioners would, *inter alia*, 'discharge ... the duties of the Board of Works'.[103] These duties, it would appear, could be assigned by order of the Lord Lieutenant or by Treasury Minute without amending legislation, or indeed, any specific reference in the Act. Section C of the Act, while essentially conferring on the Treasury the authority to reduce the functions of the Commissioners, referred also to 'Powers or Authorities created by or arising out of any former Act or Acts, and herein-after transferred and vested in the commissioners to be appointed by virtue of this Act'. The existing Board of Works (referred to frequently at this time as the Dublin Board of Works) was on the list of bodies whose duties were to be entrusted to the new Commissioners of Public Works at an early date, presumably in accordance with the provisions of the 1824 Act.

The Public Works Act (1 & 2 Wm IV c.33) was passed on 15 October 1831. The new Board met for the first time two-and-a-half weeks later, on 2 November. Almost immediately steps were taken to transfer to the Commissioners the executive functions of the old Board, which was to be closed down. The old Board attempted to frustrate the move by querying its legality. In response, the Irish administration sought the opinion of a king's counsel, Richard W. Greene, who reported, *inter alia*, 'I cannot discover any Act of Parliament creating, or defining the duration of the Board of Works; nor am I aware of any objection to its being superseded by an order of the Lord Lieutenant.' [104]

No further challenge appears to have been forthcoming. On 19 January 1832, the Under-Secretary for Ireland, Sir William Gosset, wrote to the 'Commissioners for the promotion and extension of Public Works' as follows:

> I have the Lord Lieutenant's command to state for your information that Letters Patent bearing the date the 4th day of January 1832 have passed the great seal revoking the Patent whereby Lieutenant General Quin John

Freeman, Richard French and Robert Gregory Esqrs. were appointed Commissioners of Barracks etc. in Ireland.

Directions have accordingly been given to the late Commissioners of Barracks etc. to transfer to you all Plans, Books, Documents, and other papers which may be in their possession and His Excellency desires that you will be pleased to cause proper measures to be adopted for receiving the same in your department and taking charge thereof as well as for entering on the execution of the duties as heretofore performed by the said Commissioners of Barracks and Board of Works in this country.[105]

On 12 March, the secretary of the new Board wrote to Gosset asking that the Lord Lieutenant revoke the instructions given in '1801 to the late Board of Works in Dublin, with a view to ... making such alterations by degrees in the system of its management as may appear expedient'. This was agreed to, Gosset replying to the Board on 16 March that the Lord Lieutenant had authorised it to proceed under such regulations as seemed most advantageous for that 'part of the service entrusted' to them (i.e. public buildings). He added:

After some experience in the mode of conducting this branch His Excellency has desired me to say he will be glad to have submitted to him such general regulations as you may recommend for adoption.[106]

While no copy of these new regulations has come to light, it appears that they were not as immutable as those enforced by Hardwicke, and that the terms of the delegation of authority to the Commissioners could be changed from time to time. It is undoubtedly true that the role of the Board was greatly expanded as the nineteenth century progressed. It is also true that this was done without significant amendments to the 1831 Act. This is because these duties could be assigned in three different ways, as the Crichton Committee reported in 1878:[107]

1. By other legislation.
2. By Treasury Minute.
3. By order of the Lord Lieutenant.

Thus it seems that the building function of the old Board of Works was successfully transferred *intra vires* to the new Commissioners. However, it is significant that the Crichton Committee did not spell out how the Commissioners acquired their power to build, while an abstract of legislation pertaining to the Board of Public Works, published in the early 1900s, also failed to address the issue, including only Acts passed since 1831.

It seems that with the passage of time the issue was forgotten about. There it might have rested were it not for a legal challenge in the early 1990s to the Commissioners' powers to build and manage property, mounted by a group opposed to the construction of an interpretative centre at Mullaghmore, county Clare. The matter eventually came before Mr Justice Costello in the High Court.[108] In his judgement of 12 February 1993 he found in favour of the applicants. He also found that the Commissioners were not exempt from planning permission. In his decision on 'the right to build', Justice Costello placed particular importance on the 1831 Act and subsequent legislation, and the absence therein of any reference to general building powers. He cited two pieces of pre-1831 legislation in his judgement, the 1793 Act (33 Geo. III c.34, I.) and the 1817 Act (57 Geo. III c.62).[109] The first he considered was 'not relevant, the powers therein conferred were not transferred to Commissioners established under the 1831 Act, and they were of a very limited nature'. With regard to the second, he considered that 'it terminated the Commissioners of the Board of Works, enabled the Lord Lieutenant to appoint an officer to act as superintendent of public buildings under the charge of the Board of Works, but the powers under the Act (which were of a very restricted nature) were not transferred to the Commissioners under the 1831 Act'. The judgement does not mention the 1824 Act at all (the Act designed to remedy the deficiencies of the 1817 Act and give effect to the transfer of powers), so that its status remains unclear, and possibly untested. The perceived 'right to build' loophole was rectified in the State Authorities Amendment Act (1993), enacted on 18 February 1993.

While the 1832 correspondence, cited above, refers to 'Commissioners of Public Works', the title 'The Commissioners of Public Works in Ireland' was not given a statutory basis until 1839 when it was enshrined in section 10 of 2 & 3 Vict. c. 50. Official letterheads from an early date carried the title Office of Public Works, but this was seldom used, the organisation being almost universally known during the period under study as the Board of Works, just like its predecessor, or as the Board of Public Works.[110] The abbreviated term OPW, which can be found at the head of some mid-nineteenth-century semi-official correspondence in the Larcom Papers, has not been encountered in any official (i.e. registered) papers.[111] The Commissioners were constituted a corporation for the purposes of holding land in 1869,[112] and a corporation for loan purposes in 1892.[113] The duties of the new Board were as follows:

1. The management of a fund of £550,000 for loans and grants for public works.
2. The collection and repayment of advances made out of the consolidated Fund under the earlier Acts.
3. Inland Navigation.

4. The fisheries of Ireland (formerly under the control of the Commissioners of Irish Fisheries).
5. Maintenance of certain roads and bridges (under 6 Geo. IV c.101) and the construction and maintenance of post roads.
6. Care of public buildings in Dublin.
7. The administration, maintenance and operation of the Royal Harbours of Dunmore East and Kingstown.

By 1835, £400,000 of the loan fund had been spent; under the Public Works (Ire.) Act, 1836 (6 & 7 Wm IV c.108), the Treasury was given authority to issue an additional £100,000 for public works in Ireland. Under the Grand Jury (Ire.) Act, 1837 (7 Wm IV c.2), the Board of Works was given all the powers of the county surveyors with regard to the repair and maintenance of county roads. Under a further Public Works Act, of 1839 (2 & 3 Vict. c. 50), the Board was given the powers, *inter alia*, to purchase sites for courthouses. The Board's limited functions with regards to fisheries were extended by considerable powers and responsibilities in 1842 under 5 & 6 Vict. c.106.[114]

The new Irish Board of Works had a strong engineering bias among its top management for the first sixty-five years of its existence. The decision to have an engineer at its head was first indicated in a letter written by Stanley, the Chief Secretary for Ireland, to his nominee for the post, Colonel John Fox Burgoyne, in April 1831. Burgoyne had been the officer in command of the Royal Engineers at Portsmouth since 1828. The nomination ran counter to the trend in Britain, where a successor to the Office of Works (an amalgamation with the Office of Woods) was being planned with three non-professional commissioners.[115] It has been suggested that the appointment of Royal Engineers to the Irish public service from this time was intended to provide a broadly acceptable type of professional administrator, unencumbered by associations with local politics and the Irish Ascendancy.[116] Burgoyne, who was illegitimate, had been brought up by Stanley's grandfather, the 12th Earl of Derby, in deference to a family connection.

The new Board consisted of three commissioners, rather than five as originally envisaged by Stanley. All three – Burgoyne, Brook Taylor Ottley and John Radcliff – were appointed in advance of the legislation being passed. Ottley had been a member of the Military Accounts Board, while Radcliff, a retired Royal Engineer, had lately been a director-general of Inland Navigation and a commissioner for Maintaining Roads and Bridges. Both had been based in Dublin.

Building matters were entrusted at an early date to John Radcliff, and handled by him up to the time of his retirement in 1865. Radcliff was born *c.*1799, and had a brief and apparently undistinguished military career, serving as a second lieu-

26 – John Killaly, Tullamore Gaol, county Offaly (1826-30)

Front elevation, with gate-lock entrance. A rare architectural design by Killaly, engineer to the Grand Canal Company. The builders were the celebrated canal contractors Henry, Mullins and McMahon. The gaol was built on a radial plan, derived from Limerick prison (designed by the James Pain, 1818-21), though Limerick is classical rather than Gothic. The iron railings, with their Roman fasces, may be by the ironmaster Richard Turner.
(photo Davison & Associates)

tenant in the Royal Engineers between 1822 and 1825.[117] He also found time to study law, being called to the Irish Bar in 1824.

On the professional side, the key posts in 1831 were expected to be those of engineer and architect. William Murray, architect to the old Board of Works, continued to maintain the Dublin buildings and hoped to be confirmed in office. John Killaly (b.1766), one of the two (chief) engineers employed by the Directors-General of Inland Navigation, was appointed to the engineering post.[118] Killaly had made his name as a canal engineer, serving on the staff of the Grand Canal Company between 1794 and 1810, when he resigned to take up his post with the Directors-General.[119] Killaly had also dabbled in architecture, designing at least one major building, Tullamore Gaol, begun in 1826 (Plate 26).[120]

Initially the Commissioners of Public Works left Murray and his staff of overseers and tradesmen in place. Burgoyne was not happy with his practice of employing contractors on schedules of rates, considering a system of tendering for contracts (as at the Ordnance) to be preferable. The delay in carrying out reforms may have been partly for legal reasons, partly because the Commissioners wanted to familiarise themselves with their duties. In their letter of 12 March 1832 to Sir William Gosset, the Under-Secretary for Ireland, asking for the revocation of instructions to the old Board, the Commissioners complained of the old arrangements. The Dublin Board of Works, they claimed, had met infrequently and had entrusted its authority to 'subordinates'. They now wished to bring its operations under proper control. While this remark was clearly aimed at Murray, it seemed likely there would be an orderly transition to any new system. When Killaly died suddenly on 6 April, the Board determined on another strategy – to amalgamate posts of architect and engineer and to bring in an outsider to do the job. Murray, sensing that his post was about to be abolished, wrote to Gosset seeking a retirement allowance.[121]

THE REGIME OF JACOB OWEN

The outsider was Jacob Owen (1778-1870) (Plate 27), Burgoyne's clerk of works at Portsmouth and an engineer by training. Indeed, his qualifications were essentially similar to Killaly's – early experience on canal construction and an acquired knowl-

27 – Anon., Jacob Owen,
oil on canvas

Owen (1778-1870) was appointed Architect and Engineer to the Board of Public Works in 1832 and retired in 1856. He was described by a contemporary as 'short (about 5'3") burly and balding with a florid complexion'. Owen was vice-president of the RIAI from 1849 to 1867.. (painting's whereabouts unknown; photo RIAI collection; copy photo IAA)

28 – Francis Johnston and William Murray, typical second-class (60-100 bed) district asylum

Front elevation, drawn by Murray in 1835 for presentation to the (Royal) Institute of British Architects. The seven
second-class asylums were opened in the following years: Armagh (1825), Belfast (1829), Derry (1829), Carlow
(1831), Maryborough (Portlaoise) (1833), Waterford (1835) and Clonmel (1835). (British Architectural Library)

29 – Francis Johnston and William Murray, typical first-class (150 bed) district asylum

Front elevation, drawn by Murray as part of the presentation set in 1835. Just two asylums of this type were built:
Connaught (Ballinasloe) and Limerick (opened in 1826 and 1833 respectively). (British Architectural Library)

edge of building design. As with Killaly, age was not considered to be an impedi-
ment: Owen was approaching his 54th birthday; Murray was eleven years younger.
On 26 April, the Board wrote to Gosset informing him that Murray would have no
place in the new arrangements.[122] On 9 May it presented its recommendation, to be
forwarded to the Treasury, that in appointing a successor to Killaly, it would unite
the 'two situations of engineer and architect ... by the appointment of Jacob Owen
Esq'.[123] Owen was recommended on the basis of Burgoyne's personal knowledge of
his 'abilities and integrity'. Murray was granted a pension and retained his other
official posts of architect to the Commissioners for the Erection of Lunatic Asylums
(Plates 28, 29),[124] and architect to the board of the Royal Hospital Kilmainham, but
it was to be only a matter of time before the Board of Works took over these duties
too. He lost responsibility for the asylums in 1835, and the Royal Hospital in
1842.[125] He also lost his consultancy role with respect to the design of prisons.

Owen, appointed the Board's architect and engineer on 23 May 1832, probably reported directly to Radcliff (who was in charge of matters relating to the erection and maintenance of buildings) rather than to Burgoyne, though it was the chairman, as accounting officer, who had to report in turn to the Treasury. Owen was responsible for the technical side of building matters, while Radcliff was in overall charge of the administrative side, liaising with consultants and client departments.

As has been noted, Owen was to become a major figure in Irish public works architecture, founding a dynasty that was to dominate the new Board of Public Works for almost the first sixty years of its existence. It is probably easiest to trace the legislative development of the department between 1832 and 1860 with reference to him, since he was the cause, directly or indirectly, of most of it. This was partly because while the Board of Works looked after only a limited number of buildings during its early years, Owen looked after the buildings of other departments in a private capacity until compelled by the Treasury to desist in 1846.[126] While James Pennethorne, his opposite number in the English Office of Works, had been similarly instructed in 1845,[127] it was the crisis of the potato famine and the consequent reorganisation of public works [128] that led the Treasury to demand that Owen give full time to his official duties. While other examples of free enterprise (real or alleged) became a cause for concern, and ultimately had to be legislated for, Owen successfully avoided dismissal, and eventually retired (at the age of 77), only

30 – James Higgins Owen

J.H. Owen (1822-91) succeeded his father as architect to the Board of Public Works in 1856 and died in office in 1891, just as he was about to retire.

(photo RIAI; copy photo IAA)

when he could be sure his son would succeed him.

He was born on 28 July 1778 in Llanfihangel, Montgomeryshire, north Wales, the son of Jacob Owen, civil engineer, and his wife Margaret Ellis.[129] After being educated at Monmouth, he was apprenticed to William Underhill of Tipton, Staffordshire, a canal engineer, whose daughter Mary he married in 1798. They had seventeen children, thirteen of whom survived childhood. He next seems to have worked in London, possibly for the surveyor Thomas Bush, whose military connections may have assisted Owen in his next move.[130] He joined the Royal Engineers Department of the Board of Ordnance in July 1805, and was promoted to a full clerk of works in the following year.[131] Most of his career in the Ordnance was spent in Portsmouth, where he served latterly under Burgoyne. There he was assisted in his official duties by his brother John, and in private practice by his son Thomas Ellis Owen, who had trained as an architect in London. Thomas became a member of Portsmouth corporation in 1831, and served as mayor in 1847-48 and again in 1862. He was instrumental in the development of Southsea as a watering place, designing terraces and villas.

Some of Jacob's other sons remained in England, including Jeremiah, who became a metallurgist to the Admiralty and Store Receiver at Woolwich dockyard, and Joseph Butterworth, who was the rector of St Jude's, Chelsea. Other sons joined their father in the Board of Works, where critics perceived a dynasty in the making: William Henshaw Owen (b.1813) was the Board's engineer in Limerick; Henry (b.1815) was his father's pupil and assistant before becoming surveyor for Queen's County in 1841; while James Higgins Owen (b.1822) (Plate 30), who was made a clerk of works in 1849, succeeded his father as architect to the Board in 1856. I have stated elsewhere that Enoch Trevor Owen, who joined the board in 1860 as a drawing clerk, but who subsequently served as assistant architect under James (between 1863 and his death in 1881), was another son.[132] However, he is not listed in the family tree, and it is unclear if indeed he was related. He may be the same as the Enoch Trevor Owen (son of Richard and Mary Owen), christened in the Shropshire town of Wem in 1835.[133] One of Jacob Owen's pupils, [Sir] Charles Lanyon, who received a county surveyorship in 1835, married his daughter Elizabeth Helen in 1837. The Board's senior clerk of works, Frederick Villiers Clarendon (1820-1904), married Owen's granddaughter Margaret Jane Slacke in 1853.

Most of Owen's public commissions were in Dublin, where he erected extensions and new buildings at the Four Courts (1833-40), and extended James Gandon and Henry Aaron Baker's record buildings at the King's Inns (1849-50). This was the second of two matching wings, the earlier having been constructed for the Benchers under the superintendence of Frederick Darley in 1847. Owen's earliest work at Dublin Castle was a block of castellated stables (1833) (Plate 32). He sub-

*31 – Jacob Owen, Dublin
Metropolitan Police Barrack,
Dublin Castle (1838)*

Built as an extension to Thomas
Eyre's house (1756), which was
itself demolished in the early 1960s

*32 – Jacob Owen, stable
block, Dublin Castle (1833-4)*

Detail of the crenellated breakfront. One of Owen's earliest
commissions in Ireland, it was
designed in the castellated Gothic
style to reflect the architecture of
Francis Johnston's Chapel Royal
and terrace wall, which it faces.
The stable block (now known as
the Coach House) was built on a
site previously earmarked by
Johnston's successor, William
Murray, for a screen wall. The
Coach House also served this
function, blocking the view of
unsightly buildings behind the
Castle Garden.

sequently remodelled a number of buildings there, including the State Apartments (1838-49), and extended the Chief Secretary's Office (1840-41). Among the new buildings he constructed at the castle were the Cavalry Guard House (1837) and Riding School (both demolished in the 1960s), and the neighbouring constabulary barrack of the Dublin Metropolitan Police (1838). The latter was an extension to Thomas Eyre's house of 1756, and, while mostly stucco-faced, took its floor and window levels from it. Its brick flank wall is a replica of Eyre's work (Plate 31).

The Phoenix Park was another focus for major public works programmes during the Owen era, though its management was spilt between London-based and Irish departments. A reorganisation of English departments had seen the establishment of the Office of Woods, Forests, Land Revenues, Works and Public Buildings in February 1832.[134] At the instigation of the Under-Secretary for Ireland, Sir William Gosset, who was ex-officio ranger of the park, one of its commissioners, the Irish peer Viscount Duncannon, arranged for the appointment of the London architect Decimus Burton to carry out a condition survey.[135] Burton had been employed by the old department in 1827 to design the lodges for Hyde Park.[136] Gosset's initiative eventually resulted in a major redesign of the public areas of Phoenix Park, including replanting, the realignment of the main avenue, and the construction of new gate lodges and a bailiff's house, most of the work being completed by 1842. Burton was already familiar with the park, having been asked by Dublin Zoological Society to design its gardens in 1830.[137] With the reorganisation of the Office of Woods and Forests in 1851, the Phoenix Park was vested in the Commissioners of H.M. Works and Public Buildings (Great Britain), under 14 & 15 Vict. c.42. After nine years of management by them, the park was vested in the (Irish) Board of Works in 1860, under 23 & 24 Vict. c.42. While the English departments controlled the public areas of the park, the enclosed demesnes around the official residences, and the residences themselves, remained under the care of the Board of Works. The architectural works carried out by Jacob Owen at the Vice-Regal Lodge included the east wing (1843, executed 1849) (Plates 33, 34); west wing (1854), and the coach houses (c.1842). In the mid-1840s he rebuilt the Chief Secretary's House (now the United States ambassador's residence) and its gateway, and the Under-Secretary's House (later the Papal Nunciature), largely demolished in 1986. The largest complex constructed under Owen's supervision in the park was the Central Police Training Depot (now the headquarters of An Garda Síochána), designed in 1840 and built between 1841 and 1843 by Messrs Carolin. Owen had many business dealings with the Carolin brothers, and in a curious piece of free enterprise had proposed with them to develop villas on a twelve-acre site in the north-western corner of the park in 1840.[138] This had arisen from a recommendation from Burton to the Commissioners of Woods and Forests in 1837. The offer was

33 – Jacob Owen, Vice-Regal Lodge (now Áras an Uachtaráin), Phoenix Park: alterations (c.1843)

This design for the proposed dining room, with its coved ceiling and double pilasters, was a remodelling of Robert Woodgate's ballroom of 1802. It was not proceeded with. Instead the ballroom was retained, but upgraded, and a new interconnecting dining room (completed by 1849) erected in a pavilion extension. (courtesy National Archives)

34 – Jacob Owen, Vice-Regal Lodge: alterations (c.1846)

Detail of proposed orchestra front for the upgraded ballroom (paper watermarked 1846). The Greek-revival surround includes papier maché capitals and other decorative components by Frederick Bielefeld of London. The front panel was removed in a remodelling in the early 1950s. (courtesy National Archives)

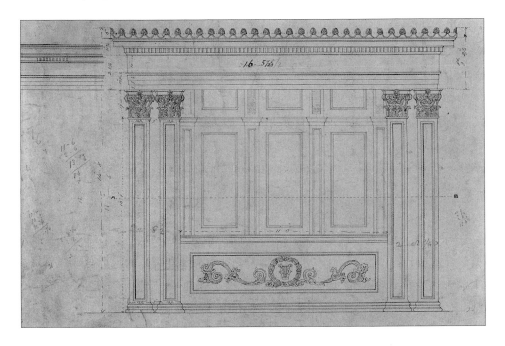

35 – Jacob Owen, Four Courts, Dublin: extension (1835-42)

Detail of north elevation of Solicitors' Building; contract drawing signed by Messrs Carolin, 1837.

The design had been prepared two years earlier, in 1835. The building was completed in 1840, but not fully fitted up until 1842. These windows lit the double-storey height Solicitors' Hall, burnt out in 1922. The façade survives as the north gable of the Law Library, but the openings have been blocked up. (courtesy National Archives)

accepted but was not proceeded with. In June 1838 a pseudonymous letter sent from Belfast to the Lord Lieutenant, the Earl of Mulgrave, had alleged that Owen and the Carolins, 'brother conservatives and orangemen', had corruptly conspired to defraud the public by using recycled and inferior materials in the construction of the Solicitors' Building at the Four Courts (actually financed by the Benchers rather than the State) (Plate 35).[139] This project had followed the erection of an adjacent block of courts and Law Library, contracted to Henry, Mullins and McMahon in 1835 (Plate 36). Owen successfully denied the allegations, pointing out that he had never expressed political views in Ireland, that members of his family supported the Whigs, and that he feared 'of all, my greatest sin is that of being an Englishman'.

Within months, however, it was not Owen, but another English architect who was to cause a stir in Irish architectural circles. This was George Wilkinson, appointed architect for all 130 workhouses to be built under the provisions of 1 & 2 Vict. c.56, the Act designed to extend the provisions of the English Poor Law to

Ireland. The Board of Works was not to be involved, due to a legal technicality, but this was not generally known.[140] In England each Poor Law union had been able to select its own architect. The Irish architectural profession was incensed when it found out, and invited Owen to a meeting in February 1839 to discuss the implications of Wilkinson's appointment. However, Owen, who could easily have been in Wilkinson's position himself, declined, and urged a conciliatory approach to the Irish Poor Law Commissioners. While they failed to dislodge Wilkinson, they agreed to found a professional body, which survives as the Royal Institute of the Architects of Ireland.[141] However, Wilkinson's achievement in organising construction of all the workhouses, many in remote locations, within the space of five years or so must have impressed his professional colleagues, who elected him to the council of the Institute in 1843. In 1851 he and Owen were appointed vice-presidents.

Consolation prizes for the Irish profession came in the shape of commissions in the mid-1840s for three Queen's Colleges (Plates 37-39) and nine new or extended district lunatic asylums, erected under the auspices of the Board of Works, all to be designed in the Gothic style (Plates 41-43).[142] A further asylum for criminal

36 – Jacob Owen, Four Courts, Dublin: extension (1835-42)

The Law Library extension, which also included new Nisi Prius, Rolls and Admiralty Courts, was carried out in 1835-38. The top-lit library was perhaps inspired by Sir John Soane's Stock Office at the Bank of England (1792). The library, converted to other purposes after 1901, was destroyed by fire in 1922 and demolished. (from the 4TH ANNUAL REPORT ON PUBLIC WORKS, IRELAND (Parliamentary Papers, H.C. 1836 [314.] xxvi. 491)

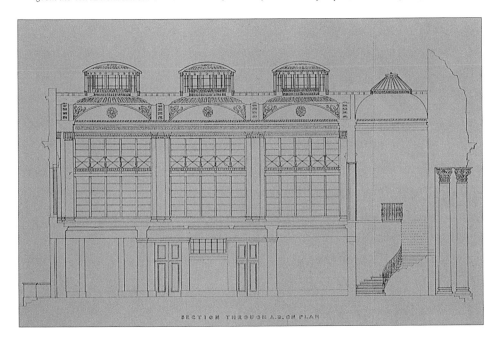

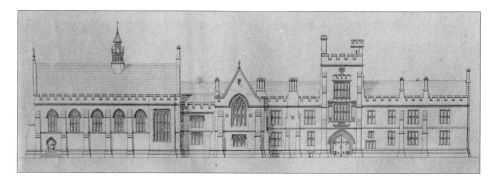

37 – Sir Thomas Deane, Queen's (now University) College, Cork (1845-49): north elevation, 1848

Deane recruited Benjamin Woodward, who was later to be his partner, to assist with the project. The main building elements – aula maxima, library and tower – were arranged on this elevation to form a picturesque composition. This and the following three plates are taken from the 16TH ANNUAL REPORT ON PUBLIC WORKS, IRELAND (Parliamentary Papers, H.C. 1847-48 [983.] xxxvii. 213). The lantern over the aula was omitted in execution.

38 – John B. Keane, Queen's College, Galway (1845-51): west elevation, 1848

Galway was the only college with a completely enclosed quadrangle. This elevation shows the residences of the president and vice-president, with the aula maxima in the centre. The main entrance, on the east side, was beneath a tower modelled on Wren's Tom Tower at Christ Church, Oxford. Architectural supervision was taken over by the Board of Works after Keane was imprisoned for debt.

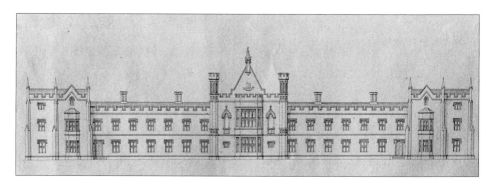

lunatics, in Dundrum, county Dublin (built 1847-50), was entrusted to Owen direct-ly.[143] The Board hoped to award a further commission, for major extensions to St Patrick's College, Maynooth,[144] to an Irish Roman Catholic architect, but unbe-knownst to them the primate Dr Crolly had agreed with the government to appoint A.W.N. Pugin, the leading Gothic revivalist in Britain (Plate 40).[145]

Owen was also concerned with monitoring the construction of the new gov-ernment prisons on the separate system, including Belfast (designed by Charles Lanyon, 1842-46) and Mountjoy (offered to Owen, but designed by Sir Joshua Jebb, 1847-50). Lanyon had come to a private arrangement with his brother-in-law, Thomas Ellis Owen of Portsmouth, to assist him with Belfast.[146] Jacob Owen had

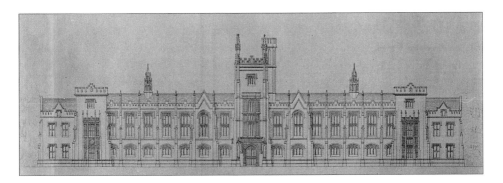

39 – Charles Lanyon, Queen's College, Belfast (1845-49): front (west) elevation, 1848

Belfast was built of diapered brickwork with stone dressings. The project was delayed due to high tenders, the design having to be simplified in execution. The double-height windows across the front of the building originally lit the examination hall, museum and library. Lanyon's clerk of works on the project, William Henry Lynn, became his partner in 1854.

40 – A.W.N. Pugin, St Patrick's College, Maynooth (1845-51): east elevation, 1848.

This is a scaled-down design, produced after Pugin returned to the project in May 1846. He had resigned the previous January after his original plans had been rejected as too costly. The two end pavilions were to house the dining hall (on the left) and the chapel. The latter was not proceeded with, and it was not until 1875 that a chapel was begun, though to a different design by J.J. McCarthy.

later engaged Thomas to draw up plans for Maynooth after Pugin resigned due to cost constraints. However, he neglected to tell his superiors, who were annoyed when he subsequently presented them with the bill.[147] The plans were by now useless, since Pugin had been persuaded to return by the college staff. One suspects a similar domestic arrangement was planned for Mountjoy; after the Maynooth debacle Jacob Owen suddenly announced he was too busy to provide drawings for the prison.

Owen also carried out private commissions, including work for other departments such as the Dublin Metropolitan Police and the Board of National Education (for whom he adopted Tyrone House in Dublin and designed the adjacent training college and model schools (1834-42)) (Plate 44). Owen continued to work for the

41 – Sir Thomas Deane, Killarney District Lunatic Asylum (1847-52)

*As at the Cork college, Deane was assisted by his future partner, Benjamin Woodward. The hospital was originally
designed for 220 patients but was subsequently extended several times. The Board of Works obliged each of the
asylum architects to design in the Gothic style, though one, Sligo (by William Deane Butler), was Elizabethan.
(photo Richard Haughton)*

42 – Sir Thomas Deane, Killarney District Lunatic Asylum: entrance front

*Like the Cork college, the design was heavily influenced by Pugin, though the style here is Early English Gothic
rather than Perpendicular. The central window over the entrance arch may be compared to that at Maynooth.
Note the contrast between the main walling material and the stone dressings. The central administrative block, seen
here, contained the apartments of the medical superintendent, the matron and a board room. As with the other
asylums, this block separated the male and female wings. (photo Richard Haughton)*

43 – William Atkins, Cork District (Eglinton) Asylum, Cork (1846-53)

The asylum was built on a steep site at Shanakiel, with three main blocks in echelon plan, overlooking the River Lee. (The photograph shows the main entrance in the central block.) In 1875 they were connected together by a pair of linking sections also designed by Atkins, making it the longest building in Ireland (over 1,000 ft). The style, like Killarney, is Early English Gothic, but Cork was a much bigger hospital, being originally designed for 500 patients. By 1904 the establishment had risen to 1,286 beds.

44 – Jacob Owen, Central Model Schools, Dublin, Infant School (1838)

Engraving c.1850; the tower was subsequently remodelled. The Infant School was the centrepiece of Owen's campus design. It was flanked by Male and Female Schools (1836, now demolished) and, to the front, the eighteenth-century Tyrone House and its matching replica, the Male Training School (1838). (illustration from P. McCann and F.A. Young, SAMUEL WILDERSPIN AND THE INFANT SCHOOL MOVEMENT (London & Canberra, 1982)).

45 – Frederick Darley, Belfast District Model School, Falls Road, Belfast (1855-57)

This was a unique quadrangular design, ranged around a courtyard. Built at the considerable cost of £16,000, it was constructed of brick, with elaborate Jacobean stone dressings and a cupola. The segmental doorcase is classical. The building was burnt out by incendiaries in 1922 and was subsequently demolished. (Lawrence Collection, NLI)

46 – Frederick Darley, Limerick District Model School (1853-55)

West elevation; contract drawing. This was one of sixteen district model schools by Darley, the first, at Newry, being opened in 1849, the last, at Newtownards, in 1862. Most were variations on this Jacobean design and were built during his tenure as architect to the Commissioners of National Education (1846-57). Many were designed with roof ventilators, often, as here, subsequently omitted from the contract. The building survives, reconstructed after a fire in the early 1980s. (courtesy National Archives)

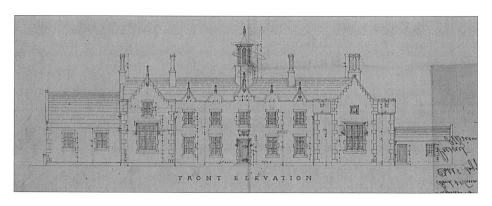

47 – Jacob Owen,
St Patrick's Church of
Ireland, Dalkey, county
Dublin (1839-43)

A competition-winning design of
1839, this is Owen's only known
Irish church. Constructed in
granite from the neighbouring
quarry, the stonework is more
sparely detailed than that of the
Dublin Castle stableblock, built of
calp limestone.

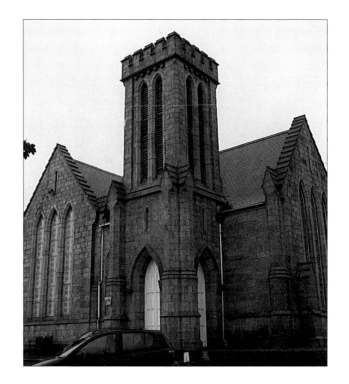

Board of National Education, until the Treasury Minute of August 1846 obliged him to give up private practice (in return for an increase in allowances). He recommended his son James Higgins Owen (then employed on famine relief works) to succeed him, but the education commissioners had other ideas, and appointed the Dublin architect Frederick Darley.[148] Darley's main duties were to be the design of a series of district and minor model schools around the provinces (sixteen or so were completed between 1849 and 1862) (Plates 45, 46), together with a number of model farms. Apart from model schools (which were completely funded by the government), the national education board was not responsible for the erection of school buildings, only for giving grants. It is likely, however, that Darley had some role in the formulation of standard designs for national schools, though very few of these seem to have been built during his term in office.

Owen's private work seems to have come mostly from public authorities, though he did design one church, St Patrick's in Dalkey, county Dublin, which won an architectural competition in 1839 and was built between 1840 and 1843 (Plate 47).[149] Owen's retirement from the public service in 1856 coincided with an impending expansion of the Board of Works' architectural activities, with countrywide building programmes for the police, coastguard, post office and education department. Owen could have retired earlier (he was by now 77), but seems to have held

48 – Frederick Villiers Clarendon, Royal Irish Academy library (1851-54)

The library (now the Meeting Room) was one of two rooms added by Clarendon, the other being the museum (now the Reading Room).

opposite

49 – Frederick Villiers Clarendon, Museum of Natural History, Dublin (1856-57)

This 19th-century view shows the present suspended glass ceiling, which concealed Clarendon's original open-work roof, with its arch-braced trusses. The classical exterior was built of granite with Portland stone dressings, harmonising with the adjacent Leinster House. The upper levels of the interior, however, are of trabeated timber-and-iron construction, with cantilevered galleries in the style of those at the Royal Irish Academy. The elevation was later copied for the National Gallery of Ireland opposite it (Charles Lanyon, in succession to Francis Fowke, 1858-64). (from C.E. O'Riordan, THE NATURAL HISTORY MUSEUM (Dublin, 1983)).

on so that he could guarantee succession to his son James, employed as a clerk of works (effectively assistant architect). James was not in fact next in line for promotion, as he was junior to the other clerk of works, Frederick Villiers Clarendon, a graduate of Trinity College who had started as a drawing clerk. Clarendon's penchant seemed more towards engineering, and he had served as secretary to the Institution of Civil Engineers in Ireland from 1847 to 1853. He had little architectural experience (other than maintenance) until he was taken up in 1851 by the chairman of the Board of Works, Richard Griffith, and one of its commissioners, T.A. Larcom.[150] Clarendon was entrusted with the design of a new library and museum (built 1853-54) at the rear of the Royal Irish Academy's newly acquired building on Dawson Street. It is not clear why Griffith chose to bypass Jacob Owen (whose

seems to have no involvement with the job),[151] though internal politics in the RIA cannot be ruled out. Griffith, a distinguished soldier, mining engineer and geologist, had been a member of the academy since 1819, Owen since 1838, and Clarendon since 1848.[152] Clarendon's RIA interiors (Plate 48), one inspired by the Great Booking Hall at Euston Station, the other by the Museum of Economic Geology in Piccadilly, were successful on both engineering and architectural terms, and led to a further commission from Griffith – the Museum of Natural History on Leinster Lawn (1856-57) (Plate 49). He also designed the curved colonnade linking it to Leinster House, as well as the Agricultural Hall of the Royal Dublin Society (1858) on the Kildare Street side. This was later dismantled and moved to Ballsbridge in the 1880s. In July 1853 Clarendon married Jacob Owen's grand-daughter Margaret

Jane Slacke. Although joining the family might have seemed to an outsider to be a good career move, Clarendon's seniority to James Owen was somewhat eroded in 1854 by the recommendations of a Treasury enquiry. This regraded their jobs so that Clarendon no longer had the title First Clerk of Works. This change effectively paved the way for James to succeed his father two years later, in May 1856. By retiring when he did, at a critical time in the Board's development, Owen could be certain that his son (who had been understudying him for some time) would succeed him.

Owen's brusque manner, family favouritism and dominance of Irish public works architecture brought him enemies. While there were several allegations of impropriety, none was proven, though it was conceded privately by Commissioner Larcom that conflicts of interest had arisen in his examination of his own pupils as candidates for county surveyorships.[153] He remained busy in his retirement, noting in his diary: 'The day is not long enough for what I find necessary to do, now that I am supposed to do nothing.' [154] He was an investor in his son's developments in Southsea, where he moved from Dublin in 1867 with his second wife Elizabeth Donnet Fry. He was a founder, with his son James, of the Irish Civil Service Building Society in 1864. He was an early fellow and vice-president (1849-67) of the Royal Institute of the Architects of Ireland. He died of cancer of the liver at Toll End, Tipton, Staffordshire, on 29 October 1870, and was buried in Mount Jerome cemetery, Dublin. Elizabeth had predeceased him by six months. He left a considerable estate, valued at over £20,000. Towards the end of his life, he set out some personal views in a diary entry entitled 'How to Prosper in Business'. Even nepotism, it appears, had a philosophical basis: [155]

> In the first place make up your mind to accomplish whatever you undertake. Decide upon your particular Employment; Persevere on it; all difficulties are overcome by dilligence & assiduity; Be not afraid to work with your own hands, and dilligently too; 'A Cat in gloves catches no mice'. He who remains in the mill grinds, not he who goes & comes. Attend to your business & never trust it to another. A pot that belongs to many is ill-stirred and worse boiled. Be frugal – That which will not make a pot will make a pot lid.

LEGISLATIVE AND ADMINISTRATIVE CHANGES 1856-60

Owen's retirement in 1856 was precipitated by a forecast increase in workload as a result of a Treasury directive. Under its terms, 'the various buildings connected with the Customs, Post-Office, Inland Revenue, national education, and other departments' were to be transferred for future maintenance to the charge of the Board of Works, the expense to be provided for in the annual estimates from 31 March

1857.[156] These newly assigned buildings included coastguard stations. To this list was added, in January 1857, the maintenance of the offices and police stations of the Dublin Metropolitan Police.[157] Owen had managed to hold on to these (following police representations) as the last vestige of his private practice. The Treasury Minutes of 26 July and 17 November 1856,[158] which transferred to the charge of the Board of Works these additional buildings, effectively transformed the Board from an essentially metropolitan institution into one with countrywide responsibilities. In recommending, in 1854, that the Board of Works should take over the architectural duties of the Commissioners of National Education, the Monck Commission had asserted that it had a large staff already employed in duties of an analogous nature all over the country.[159] This was patently untrue. There was no rural infrastructure, since hitherto, apart from what it maintained on an agency basis, the Board had only two buildings outside Dublin in its care. For the year 1857-58 a total of 559 buildings would be in its charge, of which only sixty-two were in Dublin.[160]

Clarendon does not seem to have raised any formal objection when James Owen was appointed to succeed his father. Moves to create a national structure, with a clerk of works in each province, were developed. In the spring of 1857 Clarendon and James Owen's successor as clerk of works, Charles Doyly Astley, had their titles changed to Surveyors of Buildings. Subordinate to them were two clerks of works, James Bermingham Martin Morris, transferred from the Commissioners of National Education on 1 April when Darley's Architects Department there was closed down. A third clerk of works, John Stirling, had been transferred from the site of Charles Lanyon's Belfast public offices (Plate 50). In 1858 Griffith obtained Treasury approval to appoint a fourth clerk of works to take charge of the Leinster district and to do occasional work in the drawing office.[161] The successful candidate was Frederick Franklin, formerly clerk of works to the Poor Law Commissioners. What was more significant about this competition, however, was the candidate who was placed fifth, Enoch Trevor Owen, then in architectural practice in the English midlands. The Board had written to the Treasury recommending the other 'satisfactory candidates' for other government positions, but received a negative response. In January 1859 Clarendon became rightly concerned about his own position and appealed to Griffith to write to the Treasury to obtain an increase in salary for him, citing his extra duties under the expansion. Clarendon referred to his successful projects for Griffith, the drawings for which, it now transpired, he had carried out in his own time, saving the Treasury 'upwards of £230'. He also claimed to have been passed over on Jacob Owen's retirement, though he did not criticise the Owens directly. Despite some sympathy within the Treasury, Clarendon received nothing, and while he remained on at the Board of Works, supervising the clerks of works, he never designed another building for them.

In November 1859 the Board's first drawing clerk, James Bell, retired to take up a county surveyorship. The Board proposed to fill the vacancy with one of the unsuccessful candidates from the 1858 clerk of works competition, but declined to tell the Treasury who he was until it got its approval. This was forthcoming and it was revealed that the 'gentleman ... peculiarly qualified for the appointment' was none other than Enoch Trevor Owen. He took up his post in January 1860. He was not to remain first drawing clerk for long; by 1863 had risen to the new post of assistant architect (to James Owen) and chief draughtsman. The two Owens were to run the architects department for almost another twenty years, bringing public architecture in the form of national schools, police and coastguard stations and other building types to the furthest corners of Ireland.

There is a certain symmetry in that the Dublin Barrack debacle of January 1760, that led to Eyre's dismissal in favour of Keene and the reorganisation of the Board of Works under Magill, should be followed exactly a hundred years later by another appointment controversy coinciding with further major administrative changes. While the practice of architecture may have changed in a century, human nature had not.

––––––

ACKNOWLEDGEMENTS

Thanks to Ann-Martha Rowan; to David Griffin and staff, Irish Architectural Archive; Aideen Ireland, National Archives; Felicity O'Mahony; Manuscript Library; Trinity College, Dublin.

50 – Charles Lanyon, Belfast Custom House (1854-57)

Although named the Custom House, this building was effectively the Belfast public offices, housing several other government departments and a post office. The latter was originally entered via the steps, seen here in this 19th-century view, later removed. Although the commission was awarded to Lanyon, his partner W.H. Lynn is thought to have played a major role in the design. (Lawrence Collection, NLI)

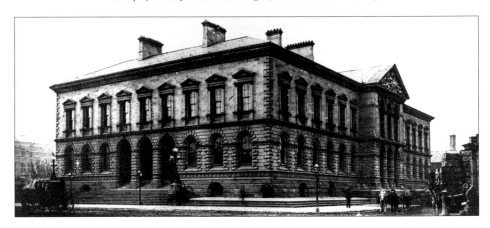

ENDNOTES

1.   For a discussion of these programmes and the architectural developments and personalities of that era, see F. O'Dwyer, 'The Architecture of the Board of Public Works 1831-1923' in C. O'Connor and J. O'Regan, *Public Works: The Architecture of the Office of Public Works 1831-1987* (Dublin 1987) 10-34.

2.   *Architectural History*, xxviii (1985) 102-23.

3.   *Architectural History*, xxxviii (1995) 91-101.

4.   E.McParland, *James Gandon, Vitruvius Hibernicus* (London 1985).

5.   R. Loeber, *A Biographical Dictionary of Architects in Ireland 1600-1720* (London 1981) 23.

6.   *ibid.*, 116-17. Robinson was in office from 1672 to 1700. He held a joint patent for the Surveyor Generalship with William Molyneux from 1684 to 1688.

7.   C.M. Watson, *History of the Corps of Royal Engineers*, 3 vols (Chatham 1915) iii, 134.

8.   E. McParland, 'The surveyor general in Ireland in the eighteenth century', *Architectural History*, xxxviii (1995) 91.

9.   E. McParland, *Public Architecture in Ireland 1680-1760* (New Haven and London 2001) 104.

10. Eyre's early career is currently being researched by Kenneth Severens, who is cited in *Public Architecture*, 13: 'Thomas Eyre started his military career in America as a cadet in General Oglethorpe's regiment and, having served as sub-engineer in Georgia and South Carolina, retired as captain from Edward Trelawny's regiment (when serving as engineer at Rattan, an island off Honduras) two weeks before his appointment as surveyor general in 1752.'

11. Opinions are divided as to whether Nevill was a victim or a villain. He was caught in a power struggle between two of the lords justices, Speaker Boyle, who represented the Irish patriot interest, and Primate Stone (a protégé of the Lord Lieutenant, the Duke of Dorset), who sided with the Crown. See E.M. Johnston-Liik, *History of the Irish Parliament 1692-1800*, 6 vols (Belfast 2002) iv, 510-12. McParland, citing unpublished research by Arthur Gibney, has written that Nevill 'almost certainly benefited improperly from contracts he entered into for barrack buildings', McParland, 'The surveyor general', 99. Dorset had signalled that Parliament should not seek the removal of Nevill as this would infringe the royal prerogative, but when it became clear that 'far from being dismissed, Nevill was allowed to sell his post for a reputed £3,000-£4,000, parliament was incensed and moved to expel him [from the Commons]'; McParland, *Public Architecture*, 136. While it is not proven that Eyre paid such a sum to Nevill, he succeeded him on 31 August 1752.

12. Johnston-Liik, *History of the Irish Parliament*, vi, 169.

13. National Archives, Dublin, Board of Works, 1/1/11. Letters patent of 18 May 1759.

14. *Observations made by the Commissioners on their views of the several Barracks throughout the Kingdom of Ireland, with estimates for repairs etc...* (Dublin 1760).

15. Anon, *The History of a Pickle-Herring or, the adventures of Butter-milk Jack* (1760). A scabrous account of Magill's career, it was presumably printed in Dublin, though the title page of the National Library of Ireland (NLI) copy (a 3rd edition) says: 'London printed: Dublin reprinted for the Worshipful Fraternity of News-Hawkers'. Magill was reputedly employed part-time as a pickle-herring (stage buffoon) with Madame Violante's company in Dublin. This pamphlet was noted by Maurice Craig (*Dublin 1660-1860* (London 1952) 169-70) but does not seem to have received any recent scrutiny.

16. *The Georgian Society Records of Eighteenth-Century Domestic Architecture and Decoration*

in Ireland, 5 vols (Dublin 1909-13) iii, 90-91; Registry of Deeds, Dublin, 192/367/128009 and 221/217/147229. He served with Charles Gardiner and other proprietors on the committee that managed the Lots.

[17] See R. Lascelles, *Liber Munerum Publicorum Hiberniae*, 2 vols (London *c*.1827) i, 106-7; 113-15 and the papers of the last Surveyor General, Thomas Eyre, in the Irish Architectural Archive (IAA), Dublin.

[18] Sleater's *Public Gazetteer*, 24-27, April 1762. I owe this reference to David O'Connor.

[19] McParland, 'The surveyor general', 96.

[20] E. McParland, 'Trinity College, Dublin – II', *Country Life*, clix, no. 4115 (13 May 1976) 1,242-45.

[21] H. Colvin, *A Biographical Dictionary of British Architects 1600-1840*, (New Haven and London 1995, 3rd ed.) 571.

[22] IAA, Dublin, 86/149, Private letter book and account book of Thomas Eyre. Eyre was still looking for compensation in 1763. He received further funds that year to pay off outstanding accounts, but had to wait until 1771 for reimbursement of the balance of moneys he was owed.

[23] *Journal of the House of Commons (JH of C)*, viii, pt. 1, xxxi. After representations to Lord Lieutenant Townshend in 1769, Eyre's pension was increased to £400, the sum he had originally computed he had lost when he left office; see Johnston-Liik, *History of the Irish Parliament*, iv, 127-28.

[24] IAA, private letter book of Thomas Eyre: Eyre to W.G. Hamilton, 25 December 1761. Funds to build the house may have come from Eyre's sale around that time of his financial interest in a development at the corner of Grafton Street and (South) King Street; Registry of Deeds, Dublin, 160/382/107932 and 176/495/119687. The house survived until the 1960s when it was demolished to make way for an office block for the Revenue Commissioners.

[25] *Sleater's Public Gazetteer*, 24-27 April 1762. Magill's post of 'comptroller' was effectively that of chief executive. He is listed in the directories from 1764 as 'comptroller of the works'.

[26] *JH of C*, vi, ccxc.

[27] *JH of C*, vi, cx. Although £14,789 worth of urgent repairs to the barracks had been identified in October 1755, only £628 had been spent from the Barrack Master's limited allowance by April 1758. A parliamentary committee report of that date stated that 'the barrack generally [is] in a ruinous condition'.

[28] *JH of C*, vi, ccxc. The granite reveals, which narrowed the openings, had presumably been inserted to allow the installation of new rebated sash boxes in place of original flush box frames or casements. Royal Square was demolished in the 1890s.

[29] Thomas Eyre, *A Reply to the Report of the Commissioners and others upon Condition of the Dublin Barracks* (Dublin 1760).

[30] IAA, Dublin, private letter book of Thomas Eyre: Eyre to the Earl of Rothes, 23 April 1760. The short time frame he envisaged for the works suggests that he was proposing repairs and modifications rather than any serious rebuilding.

[31] J.B. Maguire, 'Dublin Castle: three centuries of development', in *Journal of the Royal Society of Antiquaries of Ireland*, 115 (1985) 13-39. For Eyre's other work at Dublin Castle, see McParland, *Public Architecture*, 200.

[32] *Second Report on Historic Manuscripts* (London 1871), 3. Bedford MSS, 'Report upon the condition of the fortifications of Ireland, with plans annexed, surveyed by Thomas Eyre 1754-55'.

[33] T. Mowl, 'Henry Keene', in R. Brown (ed.), *The Architectural Outsiders* (London 1985) 82-97.

[34] *JH of C*, viii, pt. 1, lxxx.

[35] Alfray left Keene's employ in 1761 to work as overseer for the Board of Ordnance on the construction of the powder magazines at Purfleet. However, he was dismissed in 1765; see P. Guillery and P. Patison, 'The Powder Magazines at Purfleet', *Georgian Group Journal*, vi (1996) 37-52. I owe this reference to David Griffin. Alfray appeared on Keene's behalf at a meeting of the Barrack Board in Dublin in late 1765, *JH of C*, viii, pt. 1, lxxx.

[36] *JH of C*, viii, pt 2, ccccxlvii. The cost benefit analysis favourably compared the estimate with the annualised cost of providing billets in the city.

[37] *Faulkner's Dublin Journal*, 9-12 August 1766. I owe this reference to Dr Christine Casey. See also Sir John Gilbert, followed by Lady Gilbert (eds), *Calendar of Ancient Records of Dublin*, 19 vols (Dublin 1889-1944), xi (1904) 373-74.

[38] Alfray's 1767 plans of Dublin Castle are illustrated in McParland, *Public Architecture*, pls 126, 128. See also F. O'Dwyer, 'The Ballroom at Dublin Castle: the origins of St. Patrick's Hall', in A. Bernelle (ed.), *Decantations: a tribute to Maurice Craig* (Dublin 1992) 150, and 'Making Connections', 8. Myers is credited with the design of Palatine Square in Mairead Dunlevy, *Dublin Barracks: a brief history of Collins Barracks, Dublin* (Dublin 2002), apparently on the basis that he was appointed Barrack Board architect in 1767. While he undoubtedly completed the project, it is clear from the tender notice that full plans had been prepared by 1766.

[39] *JH of C*, viii, pt. 2, ccccxlvi. Compare the footprint of Palatine Square on Rocque's Map of 1756 with that on Scalé's revision of 1773.

[40] The river front of the south range was faced in limestone (presumably to match its neighbours in the Little Square), but with cut-stone at ground level. The arcades have similar ground plans on the 1756 and 1773 maps, but one suspects that the Burgh arcades were built of limestone rather than the present granite.

[41] James H. Todd, *A Catalogue of Graduates who have proceeded to Degrees in the University of Dublin* (Dublin and London 1869) 366; George Dames Burtchaell and Thomas Ulick Sadleir, *Alumni Dublinenses*, (Dublin (1935) 2nd ed.) 546.

[42] McParland, *Public Architecture*, 162.

[43] The northern leg of the west front and the reconstruction of the adjoining north range were begun in 1672, from the designs of Thomas Lucas; see Loeber, *Biographical Dictionary*, 69, and McParland, *Public Architecture*, 143. The matching southern leg and the gatehouse centre-piece, added after 1684, have been attributed by Loeber to Sir William Robinson (Loeber, *Biographical Dictionary*, 96). The centrepiece was complete by 1699 (McParland, *Public Architecture*, 145). See also John William Stubbs, *The History of the University of Dublin from its Foundation to the end of the Eighteenth Century* (Dublin and London 1889) 188-92.

[44] *JH of C*, v, 98, 181, 232; vi. 2.

[45] Craig, *Dublin 1660-1860*, 180.

[46] Trinity College, Dublin (TCD), MUN/V/5/3.

[47] *JH of C*, vi, cclxiii, no. xxxv. See also *Country Life*, xcvii, no. 2,521, 11 May 1945, 81-2.

[48] TCD, MUN/P/2/134(5).

[49] TCD, MUN/P/2/98, Letter from Hugh Darley to John (sic) Keene, 15 February 1755.

[50] TCD, MUN/P/2/100. The alterations may explain why the arches of the Venetian windows are only skin-deep.

[51] TCD, MUN/P/2/104.

[52] TCD, MUN/P/2/99/3.

[53] Engraving of the proposed elevation, reproduced by John Aheron, architect, in a pamphlet criticising it and contrasting it with his own alternative design: *Remarks and Observations on the Building carrying on for a Certain College* (Dublin 1757). Illustrated in McParland, *Public Architecture*, plate 193.

[54] A. Crookshank and D. Webb, *Paintings and Sculptures in Trinity College Dublin* (Dublin 1990) 12.

[55] E. McParland, 'Francis Andrews', in J. Ingamels (ed.), *A Dictionary of British and Irish Travellers in Italy 1701-1800* (New Haven and London 1997) 19-20.

[56] Construction of the Provost's House, under Darley's supervision, commenced a few months after the West Front (Parliament Buildings) was completed in February 1759. John Smyth has traditionally been regarded as the architect of the house on the basis of a payment of £22 15s to 'Smith Architect for a plan of the Provost's House' in June 1759. However, McParland has pointed out that a further payment of £108 6s 8d (the equivalent of £100 sterling) to an unnamed 'Architect' appears in an abstract of expenses dated about 1770. He has suggested that this architect may have been Henry Keene, since a similar sum, paid to a Mr Keen, appears in an amalgamated account (for the house and the West Front), dated 1764. On this basis, he suggests that Keene may have been employed to carry out the interior, construction of which ran on for some years after the shell was completed: E. McParland, 'An academic palazzo in Ireland: the Provost's House, Trinity College, Dublin – I', in *Country Life*, clx, no. 4,137 (14 October 1976) 1034-7. I would suggest that this hypothesis depends very much on when Keene might have been engaged, since Andrews' personal and political allegiances were with the Whigs and the Bedford vice-regal administration (which had given tacit support to Eyre) rather than the lords justices and the patriot element in Parliament. The Chief Secretary, Richard Rigby, arranged to secure a new seat in Parliament for Andrews in early 1761, a move that was challenged by one of the lords justices, Speaker Ponsonby: see R.E. Burns, *Irish Parliamentary Politics in the Eighteenth Century*, 2 vols (Washington DC 1990) ii, 314.

[57] Patrick Duigenan, *Lachrymae Academicae, or The Present Deplorable State of the College of the Holy and Undivided Trinity of Queen Elizabeth, near Dublin* (Dublin 1777) 162. The author was a disaffected academic and former board member of the college. On the face of it, a perusal of documents relating to the parliamentary grant and its surplus in 1759 (£15,000), would suggest that much of it was used in the building of the Provost's House and the rebuilding of the college dining hall, also undertaken at this time. Duigenan, however, believed that £12,000 of the grant surplus was still unspent in in 1777. This supposition does not preclude that part of the surplus was spent on the Provost's House, since Duigenan makes no allowance for the interest that would have accrued on the unspent monies over twenty years. *Lachrymae Academicae* is an attack on the character and behaviour of Andrews' successor Provost Hely Hutchinson. A lawyer and politician like his predecessor, Hely Hutchinson had all of his ambition and acquisitiveness, but none of his wit or charm. The first married provost, he had dynastic and aristocratic ambitions for his family. Duigenan blamed him rather than Andrews (who was a friend) for not completing the fourth side of Parliament Square and for abandoning plans drawn up for new student rooms (in what is now the Botany Bay area) in 1774. As Hely Hutchinson was only appointed in 1774, this seems unreasonable. If the money was really unspent, one wonders why it had not been drawn down earlier. Much of the money for the next big project, the building of the theatre (examination hall), came from the Erasmus Smith Fund.

[58] Constantia Maxwell, *A History of Trinity College Dublin 1591-1892* (Dublin 1946) 119.

59 Anon [Henry Grattan, Henry Flood and others], *Baratariana: a select collection of fugitive political pieces published during the administration of Lord Townshend in Ireland* (Dublin 1772) 292-3.

60 Johnston-Liik, *History of the Irish Parliament*, iv, 256. William Gamble MP is described as a 'hanger-on' of the Provost.

61 TCD, MUN/V/5/3.

62 Frances Gerard, *Some Celebrated Irish Beauties of the Last Century* (London 1895) 283-4. Gerard lists Andrews' pictures of Woffington as three or four portraits (rather than prints) by the London artist Arthur Pond, which she states were sold after his death. For more on portraits of Woffington, see N. Figgis and B. Rooney, *Irish Paintings in the National Gallery of Ireland*, i (Dublin 2001) 346-50.

63 Francis Hardy, *Memoirs of the Political and Private Life of James Caulfield, Earl of Charlemont*, 2 vols (London (1812) 2nd ed.) i, 147.

64 Janet Camden Lucey, *Lovely Peggy – The Life and Times of Margaret Woffington* (London 1952), 228-9

65 Instead, Robert Chapman, the long-serving overseer of the workmen, was left in charge.

66 National Archives, Dublin, minute books of the Royal Hospital Kilmainham, v, 146-50.

67 Johnston-Liik, quoting contemporary sources notes that he died on the first occasion of his attendance after the death of his only child, a daughter – 'suddenly taken with an apoplectic fit [he] dropt down dead in his place'; *History of the Irish Parliament*, iv, 128.

68 The full title of the Act was 'An Act for the Support of the Honour and Dignity of His Majesty's Crown in Ireland, and for granting to His Majesty a Civil List Establishment, under certain Provisions and Regulations'. The only bodies whose building activities did not come under the control of the Act were the Ballast Boards of Dublin, Cork and Belfast, and the Revenue Commissioners, who had authority over works approved by the Lord Lieutenant and costing under £1,000.

69 *JH of C*, xv, pt.1, 206.

70 *The Gentleman's and Citizen's Almanack* (Dublin 1788) 70. See also R. Heard, 'Public Works in Ireland 1800-1831' (unpublished M. Litt. dissertation, University of Dublin, 1977) 8.

71 For some background on Myers, Jarratt and Penrose, see F. O'Dwyer, 'Making Connections in Georgian Ireland', in *Bulletin of the Irish Georgian Society*, xxxviii (1996-97) 6-23.

72 W.G. Strickland, *A Dictionary of Irish Artists*, 2 vols (Dublin and London 1913) ii, 495.

73 Duigenan, *Lachrymae Academicae*, 162-64.

74 *ibid.*

75 J.T. Gilbert, *A History of the City of Dublin*, 3 vols (Dublin 1859) ii, 144.

76 The unexecuted fourth range, with a new centrepiece, derived in its lower levels from Richard Castle's campanile, was illustrated in Robert Pool and John Cash, *Views of the Most Remarkable Public Buildings, Monuments and other Edifices in the City of Dublin* (Dublin 1780). Chambers had resigned in 1778, feeling that he had little control over what was being erected: 'whatever merit that it has is Mr. Meyers's [sic]'.

77 National Archives, Dublin, OP 1794/509/26/9.

78 Robert Beatson, *A political Index to the Histories of Great Britain and Ireland*, 2 vols (London 1788) ii, 228. See also *The Gentleman's and Citizen's Almanack*, (Dublin 1778) 70.

79 Heard, 'Public Works in Ireland', 91.

80 *Twelfth report of the Commissioners appointed to enquire into Fees ... which are or have been*

lately received in certain Public Offices in Ireland ... Board of Works, report para. ii. House of
Commons (H.C.) 1812 (33) v, 191.

[81] *The Gentleman's and Citizen's Almanack* (Dublin 1800) 98.

[82] One of its first tasks, in July 1801, was to carry out a survey of Dublin Castle to differentiate
the buildings for which the Ordnance had responsibility. The plan is in the Public Records
Office (PRO), Kew, MPH 202, PFF123909. See also Watson, *History of the Corps of Royal
Engineers*, iii, 140.

[83] National Archives, Dublin, CSORP 1823/5033.

[84] Heard, 'Public Works in Ireland', 79.

[85] *Papers presented to the House of Commons (in pursuance of orders of 11 June 1804) respect-
ing Instructions from the Lord Lieutenant of Ireland to the commissioners of Public Works in
Ireland*, 3-11, H.C. 1805 (26) vi, 209. See also National Archives, Dublin, OP 1802/118/15.

[86] National Archives, Dublin, Board of Works, 2D/57/34. Woodgate to the Board, 7 May 1802.

[87] The extensions consisted of wings at either end of the building, housing a dining room and
drawing room respectively. These did not remain wings for long, further additions to each end
being made by Jacob Owen in 1849 and 1854.

[88] Quoted in McParland, *James Gandon*, 106.

[89] *Seventh Report of the select Committee on the public expenditure of the United Kingdom* [rela-
tive to Buildings, Civil and Military], H.C. 1810 (370) ii, 523.

[90] Blake Pinnell, 'Something for Nothing – Georgian Sinecures', in *History Today*, xliii, August
1993, 49-54.

[91] *Twelfth Report of the Commissioners Appointed to Enquire into the Fees ... Board of Works.*

[92] Under 50 Geo. III c.103 (1810), *An Act for repealing the several laws relating to Prisons in
Ireland...*, plans for new prisons had to be submitted to the Lord Lieutenant for approval.

[93] Public Offices Ireland Act, 57 Geo. III c.62 ('An Act to abolish certain offices and to regulate
certain other offices in Ireland').

[94] An offer in 1817 to secure 'a post in Dublin' for the English architect Daniel Robertson may be
connected with this Act. See Colvin, *A Biographical Dictionary of British Architects*, 822-3,
and F. O'Dwyer, ''Modelled Muscularity': Daniel Robertson's Tudor Manors' in *Irish Arts
Review Yearbook 1999*, xv (Dublin 1999) 87-97.

[95] In September 1821, rumours regarding Johnston's departure reached the ears of the architect
Richard Morrison, who arranged for Lord Powerscourt and three other grandees to solicit the
Dublin Castle administration on his behalf (National Archives, Dublin, OP 523/2). As late as
1825, Alderman Frederick Darley was lobbying on behalf of his son, Frederick Darley junior,
who had completed his articles with Johnston in 1822 (National Archives, Dublin, CSORP,
1825, 12,783).

[96] Board of Works Ireland Act, 5 Geo. IV c.23 ('An Act to amend the Act of the fifty-seventh
year of his late Majesty's reign, for abolishing certain offices, and for regulating certain other
offices in Ireland, so far as relates to the Commissioners of the Board of Works there').

[97] Watson, *History of the Corps of Royal Engineers*, iii, 141. Prior to 1793, barracks in England
had been under the control of the Ordnance. According to Watson (p.133), the alternative
arrangements inaugurated in England in 1793 were unsatisfactory, a fact recognised by the
enactment of the 1822 legislation.

[98] *The Gentleman's and Citizen's Almanack* (Dublin 1824) 220.

[99] *The Gentleman's and Citizen's Almanack* (Dublin 1825) 109.

[100] *Report from the Fourth Select Committee on the Irish Miscellaneous Estimates ... relative to Public Works, H.C. 1829 (342) iv. 127 and Report from the Fifth Select Committee...*, H.C. 1830 (667) vii, 1. See also National Archives, Dublin, OP 1829/984/4.

[101] The [Second] Duke of Wellington (ed.), *Despatches, Correspondence and Memoranda of Field Marshal Arthur Duke of Wellington K.G.*, 8 vols (London 1867-78) viii (1878) 109. Maurice Fitzgerald, *Knight of Kerry to Wellington*, 14 July 1830.

[102] A.R.G. Griffiths, *The Irish Board of Works 1831-1878, with particular reference to the famine years*, PhD dissertation 6286 (Cambridge 1968) 34.

[103] Hansard's Parliamentary Debates, 3rd series, 1831, iv, 574 (30 June 1831), and vi, 953 (31 August 1831).

[104] National Archives, Dublin, CSOLB 10.

[105] National Archives, Dublin, CSOLB 11.

[106] *ibid*. See also volume I of the Minutes of the Commissioners of Public Works (2 November 1831 – 23 June 1832), deposited in the National Archives in 1995, but uncatalogued.

[107] *Report of the Committee appointed to inquire into the Board of Works, Ireland* [Crichton Committee], *Instructions issued to the Committee by Treasury Minute*, 16 November 1877, v, H.C. 1878 [C.2060] xxiii, 1.

[108] The High Court, 1992, no. 331 JR.

[109] Reported in *Irish Current Law Statutes Annotated* (1993), 1-01, 12-01 and 12-02, and in *The Irish Reports* (1994) i, 101-65.

[110] The title of the office was given in the Dublin directories as Board of Public Works up until 1916 when it first appeared as Commissioners of Public Works.

[111] Larcom Papers. These are among the official papers assembled by Sir Thomas Aiskew Larcom during his tenure as Under-Secretary for Ireland, collated by him during his retirement, and presented to the Statistical Society of Ireland. They are now in the National Library of Ireland.

[112] Public Works (Ireland) Act, 1869, 32 & 33 Vict. c.74, s.2.

[113] Public Works Loans Act, 1892, 55 & 56 Vict. c.61, s.8.

[114] R. Lohan, *Guide to the Archives of the Office of Public Works* (Dublin 1994) 4.

[115] J. Mordaunt Crook and M.H. Port, *The History of the King's Works*, 6 vols (London 1973) vi, 181-4. The old office of Works came to an end on 5 April 1832.

[116] Whitworth Porter, *History of the Corps of Royal Engineers*, ii (London 1889) 313. Two of these engineers, Thomas Drummond and the aforementioned T.A. Larcom, served in the office of Under-Secretary for Ireland.

[117] Army lists for these years.

[118] National Archives, Dublin, CSOLB 11.

[119] R. Delany, *The Grand Canal of Ireland* (Newton Abbot 1973) 91 *et passim*, and R. Cox, 'John Killaly' in *A Biographical Dictionary of Civil Engineers in Great Britain and Ireland, vol. 1: 1500-1830* (London 2002) 384-6.

[120] His name appears as 'Engineer – John Killaly Esq.' on a plaque over the entrance to the building. The gaol was designed on a radial plan in the castellated style. See W. Garner, *Tullamore – Architectural Heritage* (Dublin 1980) 13-15.

[121] National Archives, Dublin, OP 1832/367 and CSOLB 12, Gosset to the Board of Works, 14 April 1832.

[122] National Archives, Dublin, Board of Works, 2D/57/37.

[123] *Sums paid to Jacob Owen Esq., Architect to the Board of Works, Ireland..., Contract for his*

Appointment..., H.C. 1842 [323] xxviii, 397. A transcript of the recommendation appears on p.231 of the first Minute Book of the Commissioners of Public Works; National Archives, Dublin, Board of Works, uncatalogued.

[124] For the Johnston Murray district asylums, built for the Commissioners for the Erection of Lunatic Asylums and opened between 1825 and 1835, see F. O'Dwyer, *Irish Hospital Architecture* (Dubin 1997), 10, 49-53. They were built at the following locations: Armagh, Limerick, Belfast, Derry, Carlow, Ballinasloe, Maryborough (Portlaoise), Waterford and Clonmel. Johnston's earlier Richmond Asylum in Dublin had opened in 1815.

[125] National Archives, Dublin, Board of Works, 2D/61/7, and minute books of the Royal Hospital Kilmainham, book 17, 271, 373 and 393. Murray's request for a pension from the hospital was refused.

[126] *Correspondence from July 1846 to Jan. 1847 relating to the Measures adopted for the Relief of Distress in Ireland...*, 9-10. H.C. 1847 (764) i. 1.

[127] Geoffrey Tyack, *Sir James Pennethorne and the making of Victorian London* (Cambridge 1982) 124. Pennethorne's cessation of private practice was apparently achieved by mutual agreement rather than coercion, as in Owen's case.

[128] Under the Public Works (I.) (No.2) Act 1846, 9 & 10 Vict. c.86. This Act abolished the Shannon Commissioners and transferred their functions and duties to the Board of Works.

[129] The earliest biographical note of Jacob Owen, written by his son James Higgins Owen, appeared in part xx of the Architectural Publication Society's *Dictionary of Architecture*, published in 1877. Neither it nor the account in the *Dictionary of National Biography*, xlii, 418, are particularly informative, and both contain inaccuracies. A more authoritative account can be found in Colvin, *A Biographical Dictionary*, 716-17. More recently, a short paper, 'Jacob Owen: Founder of an Architectural Dynasty', by Rosemary Dunne and Richard Trist was presented to a seminar entitled '[T.E.]Owen's Southsea – History and Conservation of a Victorian Garden Suburb', held in Portsmouth on 21 May 1994. The seminar papers, edited by Betty Owen, were printed by the Portsmouth Society in 1995. For the origins of the family and other genealogical information, I am grateful to two of Jacob Owen's descendants, John Owen and Richard Trist.

[130] I suggest this on the basis that Owen was apparently living in the City of London when his sons Thomas Ellis and Jeremiah were christened in April 1805 (Parish of St Ann and St Agnes, Gresham Street), and that Owen had a close friendship with the surveyor James White Higgins who was a pupil of Bush. [Sir] Robert Smirke was another pupil of Bush.

[131] PRO, Kew, WO 54/512. Ordnance establishment returns, 1811-14.

[132] F. O'Dwyer, The Board of Public Works, 20.

[133] I owe this reference to Sue Pike who is researching the career of Thomas Ellis Owen (source FamilySearch – international genealogical index).

[134] J.M. Crook and M.H. Port, *The History of the King's Works*, loc. cit.

[135] *Twenty-Second Report of the Commrs. of H.M. Woods, Forests, Land Revenues etc*, 1845, Appendix 10A, 39. H.C. 1845 (617) xxvii, 503. Reprinted with the original maps and new illustrations in J. McCullen and B. Arnold (eds), *Decimus Burton 1800-1881*, exhibition catalogue, Royal Hospital Kilmainham, July 1988.

[136] P. Miller, *Decimus Burton – A Guide to the Exhibition of his Work* (London 1981) 19.

[137] TCD Library, MS. 10608/2/1. Royal Zoological Society of Ireland, rough minute book, 7.

[138] Uncatalogued papers in the National Archives, cited in D. Arnold, 'Decimus Burton's Work in

the Phoenix Park, 1832-49', in *Bulletin of the Irish Georgian Society*, xxxvii (1995) 70-72.

[139] National Archives, Dublin, CSORP, 1838/1265.

[140] These difficulties could probably have been overcome by inserting an appropriate section in the enabling Act passed in March 1839 (2 & 3 Vict. c.1), but this was not done.

[141] See F. O'Dwyer, 'The Foundation and Early Years of the RIAI', in J. Graby (ed.) *150 Years of Architecture in Ireland* (Dublin 1989) 9-21.

[142] The colleges were built under the terms of the Queen's Colleges (Ireland) Act, 8 & 9 Vict. c.66. Legislation was needed for only one of the new district asylums, that at Cork (8 & 9 Vict. c.107), but the Act also provided for the enlargement of the existing asylums. The architects for the colleges were Charles Lanyon (Belfast), Sir Thomas Deane (Cork), and John B. Keane (Galway). The architects for the new asylums were William Atkins (Cork), John S. Mulvany (Mullingar), Sir Thomas Deane (Killarney), William Deane Butler (Sligo), William Farrell (Omagh), and George Papworth (Kilkenny). The architects for the asylum extensions were Murray and Denny (Richmond, Dublin), John Kempster (Ballinasloe), and Charles Lanyon (Belfast).

[143] Also built under the terms of 8 & 9 Vict. c.107.

[144] Under the terms of the Maynooth College Act, 8 & 9 Vict. c.25.

[145] Pugin had been recommended to Crolly by his great patron the Earl of Shrewsbury, see P.J. Corish, *Maynooth College, 1795-1995* (Dublin 1995) 128, and F. O'Dwyer, 'A.W.N. Pugin and St. Patrick's College, Maynooth', *Irish Arts Review Yearbook 1996*, xii (Dublin 1996) 102-09.

[146] P. Larmour, 'Sir Charles Lanyon', *Irish Arts Review Yearbook 1989-90*, vi (Dublin 1989) 202.

[147] National Archives, Dublin, Board of Works, 2D/60/11.

[148] NLI, Dublin, Commissioners of National Education, minute book, MS. 5518.

[149] *Irish Ecclesiastical Gazette*, 25 June 1872; Harry Latham, *St Patrick's Church of Ireland Church and Parish, Dalkey, Co Dublin* (Dublin 1993) 43-5.

[150] PRO Kew, T1/6222/152622. Griffith to Sir Charles Trevelyan, 10 January 1859.

[151] Royal Irish Academy, Dublin, Council Minutes viii and ix, March 1849 – November 1852; December 1852 – July 1856.

[152] Royal Irish Academy, index of members database.

[153] NLI, Dublin, MS. 7753, Larcom Papers, official correspondence on examinations for the constabulary and county surveyorships (1856/57).

[154] Diary of Jacob Owen, private collection, entry for 8 May 1856.

[155] *ibid.,* entry in 1863.

[156] *Twenty-sixth Annual Report of the Commissioners of Public Works in Ireland* [for 1857], H.C. 1857-58 [2412], xxvi, 533.

[157] National Archives, Dublin, CSOLB 262 (Govt. Letters, VIII B/5/11). Larcom to Trevelyan, 2 January 1857.

[158] PRO Kew, T1/6047A/20529.

[159] *Report of the Select Committee of the House of Lords on National Education in Ireland*. Part I, H.C. 1854 (525) xv, 1; Part II, H.C. 1854 (535) xv, Part II, 1.

[160] PRO Kew, T1/6047A/20800.

[161] PRO Kew, T1/6162A/20514; National Archives, Dublin, OPW 16839/58.

All illustrations by the author unless otherwise stated.

1 – Student drawing of a design for a mausoleum by J.V. Downes (acc 2001/156)

(all photos by David Dawson)

Irish Architectural Archive Accessions 2001

DAVID GRIFFIN AND COLUM O'RIORDAN

THE FOLLOWING IS A LIST OF MATERIAL ACQUIRED BY THE IRISH ARCHITECTURAL Archive in 2001. It includes material donated by a wide variety of individuals and organisations, and material purchased. It must be noted that while the Archive strives to provide access to its holdings, much of the material on this list is currently inaccessible, and will remain so until such time as it has been archivally processed, listed and indexed.

BOOKS

2001/001   Michael Corcoran, *Through Streets Broad and Narrow*, London 2000 (D.DUB.1.272)

Brian Dornan, *Mayo's Lost Islands: The Inishkeas*, Dublin 2000 (D.MAY.2.2)

W.A. Maguire, *A Century in Focus*, Belfast 2000 (CS.MAG.1.0)

Robert Scott, *A Breath of Fresh Air*, Belfast 2000 (D.BEL.1.33)

Lesley Whiteside, *Saint Patrick in Stained Glass*, 1997 (CS.WHI.3.0)

2001/003   Desmond Coakham, *The Belfast and County Down Railway*, London 1998 (CS.COA.1.0)

Tom Ferris and Patrick Flanagan, *The Cavan and Leitrim Railway – The Last Decade*, London 1997 (CS.FER.1.2)

Steve Flanders, *The County Donegal Railway*, London 1996 (CS.FLA.2.0)

Ernie Shepherd, *The Midland Great Western Railway of Ireland*, 1994 (CS.SHE.2.0)

Ernie Shepherd and Gerry Beesley, *The Dublin and South Eastern Railway*, London 1998 (CS.SHE.2.1)

John Turpin, *Oliver Sheppard 1856-1941*, Dublin 2000 (BS.SHE.1.1)

2001/004   David Orford (ed.), *Those Were The Days – Memories of Portarlington 1900 to 1999*, Portarlington 2000 (D.POR.3.0)

2001/006   John Blackwell and Frank J. Convery, *Promise and Performance*, Dublin 1983 (CS.BLA.1.1)
            donor: Ann McNicholl

Martin Brennan, *The Boyne Valley Vision*, Portlaoise 1980 (D.BOY.1.2)

Aodhagan Brioscu, *Irish Churches* (RP.C.85.5)

R.A. Butlin (ed.), *The Development of the Irish Town*, New Jersey and London 1977 (CS.BUT.3.0)

Fintan Cullen, *The Abbey Theatre 1904-1979*, Dublin 1980 (RP.D.310.7)

J. Forde-Johnston, *Castles and Fortifications of Britain and Ireland*, London 1977 (CS.FOR.2.0)

George Cunningham, *Burren Journey West*, Kilkenny 1980 (RP.D. 309.6)

Roderick Gradidge, *Edwin Lutyens, Architect Laureate*, London 1981 (BS.LUT.1.3)

Michael Herity, *Irish Passage Graves*, Dublin 1974 (D.BOY.1.3)

James Macaulay, *The Gothic Revival 1745-1845*, Glasgow and London 1975 (H.MAC.1.0)

Eileen McCracken, *The Irish Woods Since Tudor Times*, Newton Abbot 1971 (CS.MCC.4.0)

Seán P. Ó Riordáin, *Antiquities of the Irish Countryside*, Cork, London and New York 1979 (CS.ORI.1.0)

Restaurant Building for University College Dublin, Belfield, Stillorgan, Dublin 4, Dublin 1970 (RP.D.310.1)

University College Dublin: the Arts Building at Belfield, Dublin 1970 (RP.D.310.2)

Rural Housing in Ulster in the mid-nineteenth century, Belfast 1974 (RP.D.306.2)

Arquitectura en Capitales Europeas (1987-1991), Madrid 1992 (D.DUB.1.274)

2001/009   *Guide To St. Patrick's Cathedral, Armagh*, Armagh 1905 (D.ARM.1.7)

2001/011   Raymond Refaussé and Mary Clark, *A Catalogue of the Maps of the Estates of the Archbishops of Dublin, 1654-1850*, Dublin 2000 (D.DUB.1.273)

2001/014   Charles Dillon and Henry A. Jefferies (eds), *Tyrone: History and Society*, Dublin 2000 (D.TYR.2.1)

Tom Ferris, *Irish Railways in Colour: A Second Glance, 1947-1970*, London 1995 (CS.FER.1.1)

Tom Ferris, *Irish Railways in Colour: From Steam to Diesel, 1955-1967*, London 1995 (CS.FER.1.0)

E.E. O'Donnell, *The Jesuits in Dublin, 1598-1998*, Dublin 1999 (D.DUB.1.268)

2001/018   Brian Wragg (Giles Worsley, ed.), *The Life and Work of John Carr of York*, York 2000 (BS.CAR.2.1)
> donor: Oblong Books

2001/019   Nigel Everett, *Wild Gardens*, Cork 2000 (D.BAN.4.2)
> donor: Nigel Everett

2001/024   John de Courcy Ireland, *History of Dun Laoghaire Harbour*, Dublin 2001 (D.DUN.1.6)

2001/027   J. Frederick Rankin, *Down Cathedral, The Church of Saint Patrick of Down*, Belfast 1997 (D.DOW.2.2)

2001/032   Frank Keohane (ed.), *Period Houses: A Conservation Guidance Manual*, Dublin 2001 (CS.KEO.1.0)
> donor: Dublin Civic Trust

2001/038   W. de W. Abney, John G. Barton and R.W.A. Holmes, *Report of the committee appointed to inquire into the buildings and site of the Royal College of Science for Ireland, Dublin*, London, 1899 (RP.D 327.4)

Marilyn Silverman and P.H. Gulliver, *In the Valley of the Nore*, Dublin 1986 (D.THO.1.0)

2001/039   John S. Powell, *'Your Humble Servant': Notes and Letters from Portarlington, 1692-1768*, no. 4 in series *Documents of Portarlington*, Portarlington, 1 January 1999 (RP.D.320.1)

2001/041   N.S. Baer, S. Fitz and R.A. Livingston (eds), *Conservation of Historic Brick Structures*, Dorset 1998 (H.BAE.1.0)
> donor: Monuments and Buildings Record, Belfast

2001/042   William K. Parke, *A Fermanagh Childhood*, Belfast 1988 (D.FER.2.0)

The White House: An Historic Guide, Washington DC 1977 (BS.HOB.1.0)

2001/044   Joe McDermott, *St. Mary's Hospital, Castlebar*, Castlebar 1999 (D.CAS.7.0)
> donor: A O' Boyle

2001/045   Marigold Freeman-Attwood, *Leap Castle: A Place and its People*, Norwich 2001 (D.LEA.1.2)

2001/046   J. Mordaunt Crook and C.A. Lennox-Boyd, *Axel Haig and the Victorian Vision of the Middle Ages*, London 1984 (BS.HAI.1.0)

2001/054   Fintan Cullen, Cork, *Sources in Irish Art: A Reader*, 2000 (CS.CUL.1.0)

Vincent Kinane and Anne Walsh (eds), *Essays on the History of Trinity College Library, Dublin*, Dublin 2000 (D.DUB.1.267)

Helen Rock, Dublin, *Helen Rock's Irish Gardening*, 1999 (CS.ROC.2.0)

2001/055 Hazel Thurston, *South and South West Ireland*, London, Edinburgh and New York 1971 (D.MUN.1.2)

donor: David Griffin

Kilternan Church, 1826-1976, Dublin 1976 (RP.D.323.3)

Memorial booklet for 25th anniversary of the Church of Our Lady of Mercy, Artane (opened 27 Oct 1968), Dublin 1983 (RP.D.323.2)

2001/057 Patrick Conlan, *Franciscan Ireland*, Mullingar 1988 (CS.CON.3.0)

Lindsay J. Proudfoot, *Urban Patronage and Social Authority*, Washington DC 1995 (BS.DEV.2.0)

David Seth Jones, *Graziers, Land Reform and Political Conflict in Ireland*, Washington DC 1995 (CS.SET.1.0)

2001/058 Penelope Durell and Cornelius Kelly (eds), *The Grand Tour of Beara*, Cork 2000 (D.BEA.1.0)

John McVeagh, *Irish Travel Writing: A Bibliography*, Dublin 1996 (CS.MCV.1.0)

2001/065 Terence Dooley, *The Decline of the Big House in Ireland*, Dublin 2001 (CS.DOO.1.0)

Kevin McCarthy, *Lighthouses of Ireland*, Florida 1997 (CS.MCC.3.0)

James Morissey (ed.), *On the Verge of Want*, Dublin 2001 (BS.CDB.1.0)

Damien Noonan, *Castles and Ancient Monuments of Ireland*, London 2001 (CS.NOO.1.0)

John O'Regan (ed.), *Works 1 – James Scanlon: Sneem*, Kinsale 1995

Colin Rynne and Helen Guerin (eds), *The Heritage of Ireland*, Neil Buttimer, Cork 2000 (CS.BUT.2.0)

Kenneth Wiggins, *Anatomy of a siege: King John's Castle, Limerick, 1642*, Wicklow 2000 (D.LIM.1.12)

2001/067 Eamonn McEneaney, Dublin, *Discover Waterford*, 2001 (D.WAT.1.7)

donor: Colum O'Riordan

2001/074 D.M. McFarlan, *Lift thy Banner: Church of Ireland Scenes 1870-1900*, Dundalk 1990 (CS.MCF.1.0)

2001/075 Denis A. Cronin, Jim Gilligan and Karina Holton (eds), *Irish Fairs and Markets*, Dublin 2001 (CS.CRO.3.0)

2001/076 Richard T. Cooke, *My Home by the Lee*, Cork 2000 (D.COR.1.26)

2001/082 Michael McCarthy (ed.), *Lord Charlemont and his Circle*, Dublin 2001 (BS.CAU.1.2)

donor: Michael McCarthy

2001/086 Derval O'Carroll and Seán Fitzpatrick (eds), *Hoggers, Lords and Railwaymen*, Dublin 1996 (D.DUB.1.275)
donor: Custom House Docks Development Authority

2001/087 Cornelius F. Smith, *Newtownpark Avenue: its people and their houses*, Dublin 2001 (D.NEW.1.1)
donor: Cornelius Smith

2001/089 Christiaan Corlett and John Medlycott (eds), *The Ordnance Survey Letters: Wicklow*, Wicklow 2000 (D.WIC.1.3)

Michael Herity (ed.), *Ordnance Survey Letters, Dublin*, Dublin 2001 (D.DUB.1.271)

Michael Herity (ed.), *Ordnance Survey Letters, Meath*, Dublin 2001 (D.MEA.1.4)

2001/090 Hilary Richardson and John Scarry, *An Introduction to High Crosses*, Dublin 1990 (CS.RIC.2.0)

2001/095 John Joyce, *Graiguenamanagh: a town and its people*, Graiguenamanagh 2001 (D.GRA.1.0)
donor: Anne Henderson

2001/099 Peter B. Franz, *Jane's Letters from Ireland 1884-1886*, Durham 1999 (C.MAH.1.0)

2001/101 Michael J. Carroll, *The Castles and Fortified Houses of West Cork*, Bantry 2001 (D.COR.1.28)

2001/104 George Henry Bassett, *Kilkenny City and County: Guide and Directory*, Kilkenny 2001 (orig. 1884), (D.KIL.1.10)

2001/106 Art and architecture books (ex coll. Raymond McGrath)
donor: Jennifer O'Donovan

2001/111 Andrew and Charlotte Bonar Law, *The Irish Prints of James Malton*, Dublin 1999 (BS.MAL.2.0)

2001/112 Katriona Byrne, *Pearse Street, D2*, Dublin 2001 (D.DUB.1.279)
donor: Dublin Civic Group

Olwyn James, *Capel Street, D1*, Dublin 2001 (D.DUB.1.278)

2001/114 Philip and Delphine Geoghegan, *Building Sensitively and Sustainably in County Louth*, Dundalk 1999 (D.LOU.3.3)

Richard Hurley, *Irish Church Architecture in the Era of Vatican II*, Dublin 2001 (CS.HUR.1.1)

Seán Lennon, *Dublin Libraries: A Pictorial Record*, Dublin 2001 (D.DUB.1.281)

2001/117 Patricia Butler and Pat O'Kelly, *The National Concert Hall at Earlsfort Terrace, Dublin: A History*, Dublin 2000 (D.DUB.1.276)

2001/119 Rev W.M. O'Hanlon, *Walks Among the Poor of Belfast and Suggestion for their Improvement*, Belfast 1971 (orig. 1853), (D.BEL.1.34)

Rev R.H. Ryland, *The History, Topography and Antiquities of the County and City of Waterford*, Kilkenny 1982 (orig.1824), (D.WAT.1.8)

2001/123 Joseph Brady and Anngret Simms, *Dublin Through Space and Time (c.900-1900)*, Dublin 2001 (D.DUB.1.282)

2001/132 Kevin V. Mulligan, *Buildings of Meath*, Kells 2001 (D.MEA.1.5)

2001/133 Alex Findlater, *Findlater: The story of a Dublin merchant family 1774-2001*, Dublin 2001 (BS.FIN.2.0)

Gerard J. Lyne, *The Lansdowne Estate in Kerry under the Agency of William Steuart Trench, 1849-72*, Dublin 2001 (D.KER.1.2)

2001/140 Glenn Hooper (ed.), *The Tourist's Gaze*, Cork 2001 (C. HOO.1.0)

2001/147 Seán Duffy (ed.), *Medieval Dublin II*, Dublin 2001 (D.DUB.1.259 (2)

Emmeline Henderson, *Thomas Street, D8*, Dublin 2001 (D.DUB.1.280)

Máire Ní Chongaile, *Camden and Wexford Street, D2*, Dublin 2001 (D.DUB.1.277)

2001/148 Louis Cullen (ed.), *St. Mary and St. Michael Parish Church, New Ross 1902-2002*, Dublin 2001 (D.NEW.8.0)

donor: Louis Cullen

2001/150 John Hough, *Ireland's Co-Operative Heartland, Ardagh C.D.S – A History 1891-1974*, Limerick 1997 (D.ARD.2.0)

Gerard MacAtasney, *The Dreadful Visitation*, Belfast 1997 (D.LUR.1.0)

Jenny O'Donovan, *The Burnt Child*, Bray 1999

Maria Wooton, *The Du Bedat Story*, Howth 1999 (D.KIL.15.0)

2001/151 RIBA catalogue to early printed architectural books

2001/157 *Aspects of Leixlip*, Leixlip 2001 (D.LEI.2.1)

DRAWINGS

2001/005 Drawings of two unexecuted proposals by Robin Walker for a house at Pulleen, Cork, for Louis le Brocquy, *c.*1972 (Plate 2)

donor: Dorothy Walker

2001/020 Carton planning application report and copy drawings by Murray O'Laoire Architects

donor: Irish Georgian Society

2001/022 Lundy Collection: drawings from the offices of Henry James and Hubert Lundy

donor: Dell Lundy

2 – Proposal by Robin Walker for a house at Pulleen for Louis le Brocquy, 1972-73 (acc. 2001/5)

2001/028   Collection of material relating to the Irish Sailors and Soldiers Land
            Trust and the Iveagh Trust, Dublin (photographs, negatives,
            copy drawings, reports, etc)
            donor: F. Aalen

2001/031   Watercolour perspective view of Callan Park War Memorial, Sydney,
            by Raymond McGrath. 1925
            donor: Aidan Powell

2001/033   Sketch pencil portrait of George Petrie, dated 27 August 1851 (ex
            Jones file on Petrie)
            donor: Elizabeth Flemming

2001/034   Set of three drawings for proposed ferro-concrete bridge, Limerick
            harbour, by L.G. Mouchel & Partners, London
            donor: anonymous

2001/050   Specifications and drawings for Presentation Convent and National
            School, Carrick on Suir, county Tipperary, by George C. Ashlin,
            1881-82

2001/053   Designs of a house for Dr Lavery on Castlepark Road, Dalkey, by
            W.H. Byrne & Son, *c.*1950
            donor: Peter Pearson

2001/072   Dye-line copy set of mechanical and electrical services drawings for
            Ardbraccan House, county Meath, prepared by McCormick
            Woods Consulting Engineers, 1985-1987
            donor: Robin Mandal

2001/073   Niall Montgomery & Partners Collection
            donor: James Montgomery

2001/091   Student surveys of Gracedieu House and St John's College, Waterford
            donor: Waterford Institute of Technology

2001/097   Copy survey drawings of Leixlip Lodge, county Kildare, and temple
            and ice house at Castletown, county Kildare, by Hannigan
            Whyte & Associates Architects, Leixlip, 1975
            donor: Michael McCarthy

2001/098   Drawings (c.1870-c.1970, including drawings for Mary Immaculate
            Church, Inchicore, and St Kevin's Church, Harrington St) and
            photographs from the offices of Ashlin & Coleman Architects.
            Also, album of around thirty original drawings of church archi-
            tecture, Nuremburg, by A.W.N. Pugin, 1838 (Plates 4-6)
            donor: Roger Coleman

2001/107   Drawings and related documents concerning Ardbraccan House,
            county Meath
            donor: Marion Cashman

2001/113   Various drawings of buildings in Leixlip / Lucan area
            donor: Suzanne Pegley

2001/125   Drawings for alterations to Presentation Convent, Cashel, county
            Tipperary, 1866-1904
            donor: Kevin Porter

2001/136   Four plans for Royal City of Dublin Hospital, Baggot Street
            on loan from Eastern Health Authority

2001/142   Mounted sample decorative schemes from the firm of H. Sipthorpe &
            Co, Molesworth Street, Dublin
            donor: John O'Connell

2001/143   Framed watercolour reconstruction of the Parthenon, Athens, by
            Alfred Gresham Jones for which he was awarded a silver medal
            by the RDS, 1843 or 1844. Also, note on the building and the
            drawing by Alfred G. Jones, dated 1885
            donor: Bill Johnson

2001/156   J.V. Downes student drawings (Plate 1)
            Henry, Mullins & McMahon drawing for Clogher Palace, county
            Tyrone (Plate 3)
            Design for Wellington Monument, Dublin, attributed to Robert Smirke
            Proposed railway bridge at Westmoreland Street, Dublin, by F. Barry,
            1862 (Plate 7)

2001/169   Collection of drawings for Irish Distillers premises in Dublin, includ-
            ing the Bow Lane distillery
            donor: Irish Distillers

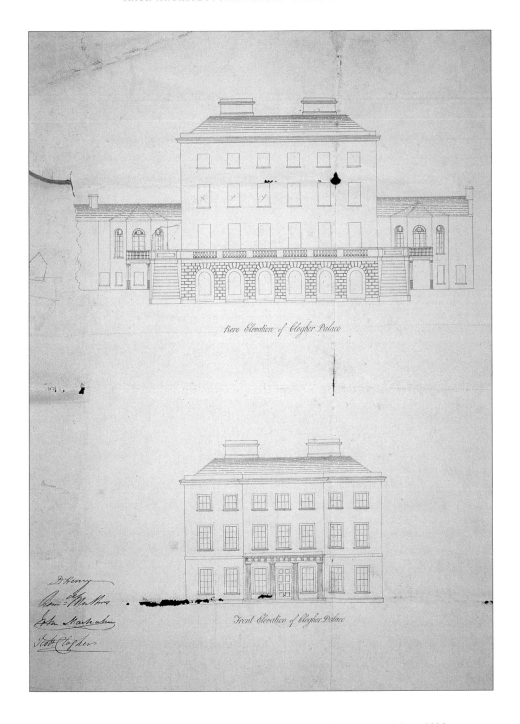

3 – Measured drawing of Clogher Place by Henry Mullins & MacMahon, 1820s
(acc. 2001/156)

church of St Sebald

Nuremberg

bases St Sebald's shrine

*4, 5, 6 – Pages from an
album of drawings of church
architecture in Nuremburg
by A.W.N Pugin, 1838*
(acc 2001/98)

186

Tabernacle St Lawrences Church Nuremberg.

7 – Proposed railway bridge, Westmoreland Street, Dublin (1862), by Frederick Barry, engineer
(acc. 2001/156)

8 – Sample pages from 'Bell Book' of James Sheridan & Sons, Eagle Foundry, Dublin
(acc. 2001/23)

MANUSCRIPTS

2001/016   Maurice Craig Collection
        on loan from Maurice Craig

2001/017   Draft copy of MUBC thesis on Harcourt terrace by Clare Hogan
        donor: Clare Hogan

2001/023   Notebook containing details of work carried out by James Sheridan of the Eagle Foundry, Dublin. The book deals with bells cast at the foundry, and provides details on location, number, metals used and tone, and also press notices of bells after installation (Plate 8)
        on loan from Kit Sheridan

2001/050   Specifications and drawings for Presentation Convent and National School, Carrick on Suir, county Tipperary, by George C. Ashlin, 1881-82

2001/073   Niall Montgomery & Partners Collection
        donor: James Montgomery

2001/084   Cantwell Collection
        donor: Eileen Cantwell

2001/085   Research files for book on James Gandon compiled by Hugo Duffy
        donor: Hugo Duffy

MAPS

2001/010   Reprint of Dublin Castle sheet of 1843 Dublin OS map

2001/059   Estate maps of Lucan Estate, Clonkeen, county Dublin (one showing old holdings and one showing rearranged holdings)
        donor: Freddie O'Dwyer

2001/060   Congested District Board area map of Ireland (large and fragile)
        on loan from Freddie O'Dwyer

2001/155   Set of bound six-inch OS maps for 26 counties of Ireland
        Also selection of other maps
        donor: Bord Fáilte

MODELS

2001/115   Early twentieth-century wooden scale model of Helen's Tower, Clandeboye, county Down. The tower was erected at Thiepval as a memorial to Ulstermen who died in the Great War, based on William Burn's 1848 design for Helen's Tower (Plate 9).

donor: Desmond Guinness

OTHER

2001/015   *Historic Heart of Dublin*, video, 2000
donor: Historic Heart of Dublin

PAMPHLETS

2001/007   *Scéal Scoil Éanna: The story of an educational adventure*, Pat Cooke, Dublin 1986

2001/013   *Conservation Plans*, James Semple Kerr, 5th ed. (ANZUK), National Trust of Australia, Sydney 2000
donor: Heritage Council

2001/021   *Architectural appraisal and conservation assessment of 85 High Street, Kilkenny*

9 – Early twentieth-century model of Helen's Tower, Clandeboye, Co Down
(acc. 2001/115)

190

Photographic survey and architectural assessment of 18-19 Duke Street and 8 Duke Lane, Dublin

Both reports prepared by Margaret Gowan & Co Ltd

donor: Margaret Gowna & Co Ltd

2001/025   *Sacred Places*, RIAI exhibition catalogue

2001/029   Building bye-laws for Dublin and Dun Laoghaire

Planning Acts 1934 and 1939

City of Dublin Pilot Scheme of Central Area Redevelopment, Nathaniel Lichfield et al

Urban Development Plans for the 1980s: guidelines for the preparation of statutory development plans, Dept of the Environment, 1983

donor: Edward Cassidy

2001/052   Pamphlet on Terenure

2001/062   Pamphlet on Cork architecture

donor: C.P. Hudson

2001/064   Dublin Corporation, *Guide to maintenance and alterations to listed buildings*, leaflets nos 1-8

donor: Edward Cassidy

2001/066   Leaflet on St Enda's Church, Johnstown, county Cork

donor: Simon Lincoln

2001/081   Printed copy of paper delivered to the Institute of British Decoration by John Sipthorpe on Dublin 18th-century decoration, March 1914

2001/093   Architectural history report on Corbalton Hall, county Meath

donor: Roger Hill

2001/094   Raheny Heritage Trail, 2000

donor: Flynn John Architects

2001/100   Guide to St Doulough's Church

2001/110   National Inventory of Architectural Heritage volumes for Roscommon, Roscrea, Sligo, Monaghan, Cavan, Castlebar and Carrick on Shannon

donor: Dúchas, The Heritage Service

2001/116   Copy of article on Delville, Glasnevin, county Dublin, by H. Elrington from *The Connoisseur*, October 1924

donor: Knight of Glin

2001/121   Guide book for Mount Stewart gardens

2001/134   Pamphlet on Georgian house and garden, Limerick

donor: Limerick Civic Trust

2001/137   Rory Murphy, *Battle of Newtownbarry*, Bunclody 1998
             donor: Michael Cowman

2001/138   Commissioned house histories for Garrykennedy House, county
             Tipperary, and No. 45 Wellington Road, Dublin, produced by
             Eleclann Ltd
             donor: Eleclann

2001/144   Report on eighteenth-century Irish gates and gatelodges prepared by
             John Redmill for George Mangan, 1999
             donor: George Mangan

2001/149   Short history of St Cartha's RC church, Kilcar, county Donegal, by
             Catherine Campbell
             donor: Catherine Campbell

2001/154   Historic building reports on Hollywood House and Cedarwood House,
             Mount Anville, Dublin, Gentian House, Galway, and No. 43
             Eyre Square, Galway, by Robin Mandal
             donor: Robin Mandal

2001/170   Mary Johnston, local history thesis on Bishop's Court, county Kildare
             donor: Mary Johnston

2001/172   Collection of pamphlets on individual churches in Northern Ireland
             donor: Dick Oram

PERIODICALS

2001/078   *Bulletin of the Institution of Civil Engineers*, *c.*1931-69 (duplicates)
             donor: National Library of Ireland

2001/088   Run of *Old Kilkenny Review*, mid 1970s to 2001 (incomplete run)
             donor: John Kirwan

2001/118   Run of *Journal of the Society of Architectural Historians*, 1950s to
             1970s (also, cuttings relating to American architecture)
             donor: Rory O'Cuive

PHOTOGRAPHS

2001/016   Maurice Craig Collection
             on loan from Maurice Craig

2001/026   Colour photographs of Clochristy, county Carlow, by John Kirwan
             donor: John Kirwan

2001/028   Collection of material relating to the Irish Sailors and Soldiers Land
            Trust and the Iveagh Trust, Dublin (photographs, negatives,
            copy drawings, reports, etc)
            donor: F Aalen

2001/030   Copy photograph of Masonbrook, county Galway
            donor: Gordon Mark

2001/040   Two albums of photographs and press cuttings relating to Charleville
            Castle and Tullamore, and Dublin city and southern suburbs
            donor: Kevin Harrington

2001/049   Colour photographs (2) of stained-glass window, Farnaght church,
            Mohill, county Leitrim
            donor: Petra Coffey

2001/051   Paddy Healy Collection
            donor: Paddy Healy

2001/061   J.V. Downes Glass Lantern Slide Collection
            donor: UCD Architecture Library

2001/064   Colour photographs of Dalkey, county Dublin (2), and Enniscorthy,
            county Wexford (7)
            donor: Edward Cassidy

2001/077   Mangan Collection, copy photographs from the Mangan Biddluph
            photograph albums
            donor: Offaly Historical Society

2001/083   Copy photographs of Church of Ireland College of Education, Kildare
            Place
            donor: Church of Ireland College of Education

2001/105   Various photographic prints (ex coll. Edward Cassidy)

2001/108   Photographic prints by Richard Dann
            donor: Richard Dann

2001/126   Photographs of St John's Church of Ireland, Sligo; tower, Shell Cottage
            and entrance front, Carton, county Kildare c.1870

2001/145   *Buildings of Ireland*, photographic negatives
            on loan from Alistair Rowan

2001/159   Miscellaneous collection of reports, colour photographs and slides
            donor: Cathal Crimmins

2001/161   c.1,000 photographs of buildings in N. Ireland by Kieran Glendinning
            donor: Kieran Glendinning

2001/163   Photographs of designs for gates and gate lodges, Westport, county
            Mayo by Henry Holland and J.B. Papworth
            donor: J.A.K. Dean

2001/166   Photographs of the Church of Our Lady of the Wayside, Kilternan, county Dublin, taken by the late Pat Johnston
donor: Mairead Johnston

2001/175   Copy of photograph of RDS Lecture Theatre (Dáil Chamber), Leinster House, under construction
donor: Mary Kellegher

PLANNING REPORTS

2001/047   Planning permission report on external improvements and refurbishment, No. 51 St Stephen's Green, Dublin 2
required deposit: Building Design Partnership (BDP)

2001/048   Additions and corrections to inventory of Loreto Abbey, Rathfarnham, Dublin 14 (to be inserted into original inventory ACC 2000/172)
required deposit: Frank Benson & Partners Architects

2001/056   Planning permission survey of proposed Dunnes Stores office and retail development, Upper Stephen Street / South Great George's Street, Dublin, by Arthur Gibney and Dublin Civic Trust
donor: Dublin Corporation

2001/070   Report on No. 3 Pim Street, Dublin 8, prepared by William Doran, architect, as a condition of planning permission
required deposit: Frank McGill

2001/071   Report on No. 47 Mount Pleasant Avenue Upr, Dublin 6, prepared by Gerrard Kennedy as a condition of planning permission
required deposit: Gerrard Kennedy Architect

2001/080   Architectural and historical report on No. 19 Temple Gardens, Rathmines, Dublin 6, prepared in accordance with planning permission decision by Bluett & O'Donoghue Architects, 14 Dec 2000
required deposit: Bluett & O'Donoghue Architects

2001/103   Planning permission report on GPO by Kavanagh Tuite Architects, 2001
required deposit: Kavanagh Tuite Architects

2001/131   Planning permission submission in relation to No. 60 Thomas Street, Dublin
required deposit: Holohan Architects

2001/139   Planning permission report on No. 28 Thomas Street, Dublin
required deposit: Cathal Crimmins

———

Shorter Notices

1 – Thomas Mitchell (attrib.) A View of Kilkenny, c.1757, oil on canvas, 95 x 150.5 cm
(courtesy National Gallery of Ireland)
2 – Thomas Mitchell, A View of the River Boyne with gentlemen and horses by a statue to
William III in the foreground, the Boyne Obelisk beyond, 1757, oil on canvas, 107 x 175.5cm
(collection Ulster Museum; courtesy Trustees of the Museums & Galleries of Northern Ireland)

A View of Kilkenny

NICOLA FIGGIS

I N THE COURSE OF PREPARING THE CATALOGUE OF *PAINTINGS OF THE IRISH SCHOOL in the National Gallery of Ireland*, volume I, with Brendan Rooney (NGI 2001), this extensive view of Kilkenny (cover, Plate 1),[1] at that time categorised as Irish School,[2] came under considerable scrutiny. Technical examination by the conservation department revealed that the artist had used a distinctive red underpaint to sketch in outlines of the composition. This particular technique can also be seen in Thomas Mitchell's painting *A View of the River Boyne with gentlemen and horses by a statue to William III in the foreground, the Boyne Obelisk beyond*, signed and dated 1757 (Ulster Museum) (Plate 2). Other aspects of the paintings show strong similarities: the placing of figures and horses in relation to the background, and the treatment of foliage, especially of hanging ivy. On the basis of these comparisons, the National Gallery's *A View of Kilkenny* is now attributed to Thomas Mitchell.

Thomas Mitchell (1735-1790), an English artist who worked as a shipwright in the British Admiralty and held a position in the dockyard at Chatham, is usually known for his marine paintings. He visited Ireland in 1757, when he painted the Ulster Museum landscape, and produced another of Sir John and Lady Freke with Mr Jeffreys of Blarney by a lake.[3] It is most likely that he painted the National Gallery's *A View of Kilkenny* in the same year.

ENDNOTES

[1] NGI 4467; oil on canvas, 95 x 150.5 cm; provenance: 7th Marquess of Ormonde and the Trustees of the Ormonde Settled Estates; purchased 1983 as attributed to William Ashford.

[2] For a detailed description of the painting, see *National Gallery of Ireland: Acquisitions 1982-83* (Dublin 1984) 20-1.

[3] Eileen Black, *Irish Oil Paintings, 1572-c.1830* (Belfast 1991) 49; Ellis Waterhouse, *British 18th Century Painters* (Woodbridge 1981) 242.

A database of Irish architects 1720-1940: progress report

ANN MARTHA ROWAN

AT THE IRISH ARCHITECTURAL ARCHIVE IN DUBLIN, I AM COMPILING A DATA-base of Irish architects and their works. The project was described in the *Bulletin of the Irish Georgian Society*, xxxvi (1994) 75-7. For a few years lists of the persons included in the database were published in the *Bulletin* and, subsequently, in the journal of the Irish Georgian Society, *Irish Architectural and Decorative Studies*. The most recent of these lists, covering the letters E and F, appeared in 2000 in volume 3 of *Irish Architectural and Decorative Studies*.

I believe, however, that publication of the lists is not particularly useful because the information in them is constantly being changed and because they have always lagged far behind the progress which has actually been made. Instead, therefore, a note of progress made will be placed in the journal each year. At this moment (November 2002) inputting has reached the letter S, or more specifically SM, as in Smith.

Irish Georgian Society

CONSERVING IRELAND'S ARCHITECTURAL HERITAGE

THE IRISH GEORGIAN SOCIETY AIMS TO ENCOURAGE AN INTEREST IN AND TO promote the preservation of distinguished examples of architecture and the allied arts in Ireland. These aims are achieved by:

■ MEMBERSHIP – The Society has 3,000 members worldwide. Its headquarters are in Dublin, and there is a thriving and long-established London Chapter and two local Irish chapters in Birr and Limerick. The headquarters of the US membership, IGS Inc., is in New York, and there are local chapters in Boston, Chicago, Cleveland, Columbus, Washington, Minneapolis and Atlanta. The benefits of membership include: (i) a twice-yearly newsletter which includes the events programme; (ii) the annual journal; (iii) free entry to selected historic houses in Ireland.

■ FUNDRAISING – The Society runs an events programme which includes: (i) lectures, (ii) private theatre evenings, (iii) architectural walking tours, (iv) conferences and seminars, (v) day tours, including visits to houses not normally open to the public, and (vi) tours abroad.

■ EDUCATION – The Society's annual journal, which has been published regularly since 1958, contains articles of original research, and is the only Irish periodical devoted entirely to the architectural history of Ireland. In addition, valuable research in the field of conservation is funded by the Desmond Guinness Scholarship.

■ GRANTS – Donations to the Society and funds raised through the events programme enable the Society to make grants towards the restoration of historic properties.

■ PLANNING PARTICIPATION – The Society takes an active part in the planning process on a country-wide basis, and opposes planning applications which are not compatible with the principles of good conservation. It also provides general advice on other aspects of conservation.

The Society liaises with government departments in the area of conservation. The Government has accepted that the preservation and conservation of Ireland's historic buildings, precincts, properties and collections should be given high priority.

HISTORY

The Irish Georgian Society was founded in 1958 by the Hon Desmond Guinness and his late wife, Mariga, for the protection of buildings of architectural merit in Ireland. Many fine houses have been saved through their enthusiasm and commitment, and the dedication of members and supporters. The current President is Desmond FitzGerald, Knight of Glin.

The Society's main achievements include, among others, the saving of threatened great buildings such as: Castletown, county Kildare; Damer House, county Tipperary; Doneraile Court, county Cork; Roundwood, county Laois; Tailors Hall, Dublin, and 13 Henrietta Street, Dublin. Restoration work is being carried out at Ledwithstown, county Longford, and Mount Ievers Court, county Clare, and the Society is assisting with the urban restoration at 2 Pery Square, Limerick. The Society has provided grants for many other projects, including the restoration of correct windows in historic urban houses, such as 20 Lr Dominick Street, George Bernard Shaw's house in Synge Street, and 3-4 Fownes Street, Dublin.

These efforts are funded by our members' participation in the events programme, by the fundraising activities of our chapters, by donations, by sales from the Society's book and gift shop, and by generous royalties from Kindel & Co Inc., Scalamandre Inc., Chelsea House, and the Obelisk Collection.

MEMBERSHIP APPLICATION

Membership application forms are available from:

IRISH GEORGIAN SOCIETY
74 Merrion Square, Dublin 2
tel: +353 (0)1-676 7053 / fax: +353 (0)1-662 0290 / e-mail: info@igs.ie

Arthur Prager, Executive Director
IRISH GEORGIAN SOCIETY INC.
7 Washington Square North (21A), New York, NY 10003 6647
tel: (212) 254 4862 / fax: (212) 777 6754 / e-mail: irgeorgian@aol.com

Back-Issues

IRISH ARCHITECTURAL AND DECORATIVE STUDIES

THE JOURNAL OF THE IRISH GEORGIAN SOCIETY – VOLUME I, 1998

IRISH ARCHITECTURAL AND DECORATIVE STUDIES

THE JOURNAL OF THE IRISH GEORGIAN SOCIETY – VOLUME II, 1999

BACK-ISSUES

IRISH ARCHITECTURAL AND DECORATIVE STUDIES

THE JOURNAL OF THE IRISH GEORGIAN SOCIETY – VOLUME III, 2000

IRISH ARCHITECTURAL AND DECORATIVE STUDIES

THE JOURNAL OF THE IRISH GEORGIAN SOCIETY – VOLUME IV, 2001

SHORTER NOTICES

Back-issues of *Irish Architectural and Decorative Studies* are available from the Irish Georgian Society and Gandon Editions (for contact information, see page 4).